great
protestant
festivals

great

protestant

festivals

· clarence seidenspinner

 henry schuman · n. y.

to gilbert · our son

to roberta · our daughter

contents

foreword

This book has been written for all people who are interested in the worship of the Protestant Church. Here is the story of what actually happens in the parish churches of the major Protestant denominations during the annual cycle of worship. It is a book for layman and church school workers, for ministers and students who want to have a comprehensive picture of how the liturgical year comes and goes. It is a book, too, for Catholics and non-churchmen and all who want to understand the mystery, beauty and design of Protestant worship.

This book is a record and reflection of existing patterns. An occasional liturgical scholar may protest, "Don't you know that the liturgical year begins with Advent? You have made it begin in September." Of course, the author knows that simple fact. All the pastors and laymen of Protestantism know, however, that the church begins with summer's end. That is when people return from their vacations and settle down to the program of the new church year. That is the reason why

foreword

Protestant worship has been described in terms of the four seasons of the year. That is the way the church year is planned and set up in actual practice in the parish church.

It is the author's hope that this book, not only may describe how Protestant churches worship during the year, but also, may stimulate interest in experimentation, the enrichment of parish programs and the encouragement of ever new designs and services. To this end, the seasonal program of specific churches is often described.

The author is happy to take this opportunity to express his great appreciation for the help of his secretary, Miss Gladys Reep, in the preparation of the manuscript, and to all the churches and pastors whose parish practice has provided the information that made this book possible.

great
protestant
festivals

· festive worship in protestant churches

Everyone loves a party! What fun it is to celebrate a birthday with gaily wrapped packages, good friends and a huge cake all glistening in its very own candlelight! What fun it is, on a holiday, to pack a picnic basket, invite the neighbors to share the day, and to go off to the woods or the beach! Everyone likes to mark a special occasion by some kind of a celebration. Everyone likes to put a halo around life's festive moments.

No wonder that Protestant Christians enjoy the yearly cycle of worship. It binds the festive days together into a dramatic movement, with moments of thrilling climax. When summer vacation days are over and the world squares up to normal, children and their parents, young people and adults, look forward to Rally Day at the church. This is a warm-hearted homecoming when friends greet one another again. Summer has gone by; people have gone north and south, east and west, on vacations of all kinds. They are glad to come back home at the end of summer and to find their security once more in the fellowship of familiar faces and voices. Rally Day is the time when nearly everyone is back home and when hands are clasped in greeting and good wishes. Rested bodies and exhilarated minds are ready to meet one another for the fellowship of worship and study, work and play, for the new church year.

Other festive days brighten the autumn season. Presently World Communion Sunday comes to remind each parish church that it does not stand alone in the community and that its denomination does not work alone in the world. World Communion Sunday reminds each parish church that it is part of the larger fellowship of Christians who are at work throughout the world in many different ways, but who are united in their loyalty to God and their devotion to the church. World Communion Sunday helps Christians to understand that no matter what their denominational affiliations may be, they are members of what the historic creeds call, "The Holy Christian Church," or, "The Holy Catholic Church."

The autumn season brings other festal days: Thanksgiving with its service of the harvest festival, its homecomings, its family dinners. After Thanksgiving has passed, Christmas is just around the corner. It comes with all the glistening gaiety and memoried beauty and celebration which all the world loves. Just a week later Protestant Christians go to their parish church to celebrate Watch Night or the beginning of the new year. Hearts are still keyed to a high pitch because of the wonder of Jesus, set forth during Christmastide, and the hope which they have in Him as they look forward to the new year.

The first of the year good Christian hearts look forward to the Easter cycle which begins with Lent. This is the season of penitence and sacrifice, of additional study, and greater attention to worship. It reaches climactic movement in the historic events and services of Holy Week, when each Christian follows his Lord through those events set forth in the Passion stories of the gospels. The great climax is reached upon Easter itself, when the Festival of the Resurrection is celebrated for seven weeks. Then Eastertide reaches its second climax in the Festival of Pentecost, which is the birthday of the church.

These are the great days around which the church year is formed. These days are the golden, crimson bands in the rich tapestry of Protestant worship. Other days there are in abundance: days like Brotherhood Sunday and Memorial Day, the Festival of the Christian Home and Rural Life Sunday, all of them adorning the yearly pattern of worship with their own color and interest and significance. They are satelite days which revolve around the major festivals just as the planets revolve around the sun.

It is sometimes said that Protestant worship lost its joy and beauty because the liturgical year, or calendar of worship, in the older churches was laid aside by the reformers. Actually, this was never really true. Much of the beauty of ancient worship continues to characterize the major branches of Protestantism. In Germany, the transition from Roman Catholic worship to

Lutheran worship was very easy. For the most part, the only changes made were the translations of the service into the vernacular, particularly that of the daily office used on Sunday morning and the slight shift in the theological basis of the mass or Holy Communion. In the Roman service the corporeal presence of Christ was effected during the celebrant's prayer of consecration by the miracle of transubstantiation. In the Lutheran service the change from the bread and wine of Holy Communion into the real presence of Christ was effected through the faith of the believers in the process known as consubstantiation. The shift, in other words, was from the mechanical reading of the service to the necessity of faith on the part of the congregation. Some of the saints' days in the calendar of worship were deleted, stirring congregational singing was introduced and the preaching of the gospel was given new importance. Indeed, Luther spoke of the sermon as having a sacramental importance in that it, as well as Holy Communion, was a means of grace. Otherwise, Divine Worship remained much the same for the German Lutherans as it had been during their Catholic days.

In Switzerland further changes were made in Zurich under the leadership of Zwingli. There Holy Communion was reduced to a memorial meal and was celebrated only occasionally. The beauty of Catholic worship, together with its rich ceremonial and magnificent music was eliminated in favor of a stark, austere service which emphasized the reading and the interpretation of the Bible.

In England the transition from Roman Catholic worship to Episcopalian or Anglican worship was more like the Lutheran movement than the Reformed movement of Switzerland. The structure of the daily office and the liturgy of Holy Communion, together with the yearly cycle of worship remained much the same as it had been in Catholic practice. To be sure, the number of daily offices was reduced to two, namely, matins and evensong. In the minds of the Protestant sector of the Anglican Church the prayer of consecration was divested of its transubstantiation implications. Some of the saints' days and those devoted to the honor of the Virgin Mary were eliminated. For the most part, Anglican worship was changed only at those points where Lutheran worship was changed, though there was less emphasis in England among the Episcopalians upon the sermon than there was among the German Lutherans. The English reformation among the Episcopalians represented more of an administrative break with Rome than a liturgical one.

Even among the Puritans, the most austere of Protestant groups, the glory of Sunday worship was retained. Every Sunday was a little Easter and was called the Lord's Day, to designate it as a memorial of the resurrection of Jesus on the first day of the week. To be sure, for many years, in austere Protestant circles, festal days like Christmas and Easter were not observed. Nevertheless, during the weekly celebration of Divine Worship, the New Testament was bound to be read in something of its entirety, and in one way or another the memory of the great festive days thus kept.

Too often we are inclined to equate the Protestant movement with the Puritan expression of Christianity. We must always remember that the Lutheran population of Germany and the Anglican population of Great Britain were large and that the Puritan movement was only a part of the Reformation.

Today, as never before, Protestant worship is a succession of festal days. The old observances take their familiar places as the great and comforting suns in the liturgical world. They serve to brighten the new days which Protestant Christianity has added to the annual cycle of worship: days like Rally Day and Children's Day, World Communion Sunday and the Festival of the Reformation, and many others which we shall discuss later.

Of course, there are many differences in the practice of Protestant worship because there are so many denominations, 221 in fact. These denominations range all the way from the dignified Episcopalians to the shouting members of certain Pentecostal groups. Nevertheless, it is not as difficult as one might imagine to find the Protestant norm of worship. According to a 1951 news service report on Protestant membership, published by the National Council of Churches of Christ in America, 76% of all Protestant Christians are in churches of one million or more members. Some of these groups, like the Methodist, are very large, numbering about nine million. 95% of all Protestant Christians are in those 38 denominations which have 100,000 or more members each.

Since most of the larger bodies are members of the

National Council, and are thus united in essential spirit, we shall use their general practices as a norm of Protestant worship. It would take too long a book to describe the yearly cycle of all 221 denominations classified as Protestant. This would make an interesting excursion into the worship of Christians but we do not have time for it in this book. We must confine ourselves to the general practice of the major bodies. The great Protestant festivals that we describe will characterize the worship of a very substantial Protestant majority.

Rally Day: doors swing open for this autumn observance. Episcopalians and Lutherans, Methodists and Presbyterians, Baptists and Congregationalists, and all the other Protestant Christians hear the sound of the church bell on that eagerly awaited day. They make their way to their respective parish churches to settle down for another year of worship together. Soon the Christmas wreaths are hung in the nave and the beautiful carols are sung again. Even while Christmas is being celebrated, the Easter cycle is all but here. Soon Easter altars and communion tables will be adorned with lilies and, when that happens, Pentecost is nearly here and children and adults are looking forward to their confirmation into the membership of the church. Each year it is much the same and in this yearly cycle of worship Protestant Christians find comfort and security.

CHAPTER TWO

• ## protestant worship and tradition

Even in the long ago, when there was but one Catholic and Apostolic Church, the calendar of worship varied greatly. East and West did not always agree. In the Eastern churches, which looked for leadership to such metropolitan centers as Antioch, Alexandria and Constantinople, a tradition of worship developed which was based upon some of the earliest practices of the Christian community.

Originally the church year in worship began with Easter itself. This festival was known as Pascha, a name reminiscent of the Jewish festival celebrated simultaneously. Soon, however, the opening day of the church year was changed to the Feast of the Holy Cross which came during the middle of September. The Western church, however, began its year with Advent which generally opened on the first Sunday in December. Furthermore, this Western season of Advent was shorter than the one observed in the East where the opening day came earlier. Even the Nativity date of East and West did not coincide. The Eastern churches tended to celebrate the Nativity on January 6 while Western churches seemed to favor the 25th of December.

Since these differences were apparent even before the great schism between East and West in the 11th century, it should not surprise us to discover Protestants using the same principles of selection in their attitude toward the traditional calendar of Roman Catholic Christianity.

What is the attitude of the Protestant Church toward the traditional calendar of worship? Does Protestantism have any standard by which to evaluate traditional worship and select those parts of it which are in harmony with Reformation? These questions are fundamental if we are to understand the difference between the great Catholic and the great Protestant festivals.

To outline the whole Roman calendar of worship, or even to describe its high spots, would be to repeat what James L. Monks, S.J., has done so well in his book on "Great Catholic Festivals." Suffice it to say that Catholic worship centers in the celebration of the mass. At the heart of this service was the theological and devotional faith in the real presence of Christ upon the altar following the prayers of consecration.

Certain portions of the mass are variable and are known as the proper of the season. In introits, psalms, scripture lessons and collects, the changing nature of the church year is set forth. This year begins with Advent in preparation for the first festival of the Deity which is Christmas. Christmastide moves through a twelve day period to Epiphany which is the celebration of the manifestation of Jesus to the Gentile world. Epiphanytide moves along to the three Sundays preceding Lent, Sundays known as Septuagesima, Sexagesima and Quinquagesima. Lent begins on Ash Wednesday, forty days before Easter, not counting the Sundays. It is followed by the second festival of the Deity, that of the resurrection known as Easter. Eastertide lasts for seven weeks when the third festival of the Deity is celebrated, that of Pentecost. In the Roman calendar, all of the other Sundays until Advent are known as Sundays after Pentecost. Within their cycle the fourth festival of the Deity occurs, the Sunday after Pentecost. It is known as Trinity Sunday.

Adorning this basic structure of the church year were various saints' days and other festivals, including those devoted to the memory and exaltation of Mary. These included such festivals as The Annunciation, The Purification, The Presentation, The Assumption and others. There are seventeen of these festivals of Mary observed by the Catholic Church. Outward and visible expression of this esteem for Mary is shown in the superb paintings and architecture devoted to her exaltation. Think of the great madonnas of the Renaissance painters! Think of the great parish churches and cathedrals dedicated to her name, such churches as Notre Dame in Paris, and others! All of these outward and visible hymns of praise to Mary are but the visual manifestations of Catholic devotion to her name which find expression in the liturgical cycle.

· 21

Meanwhile, a number of days in Catholic worship are devoted to saints and martyrs of the church. Their intercession before the heavenly throne is often formally sought. This practice was developed by some of the great church fathers such as John Chrysostom. When he preached on Saints Bernice and Prosdace, for example, he urged his congregation to seek their intercession, "For they have great boldness, not merely during their life, but also after death, yea, and much greater after death. For they now bear the stigmata of Christ, and when they show this, they can persuade the King to anything."

Concerning this complex calendar of worship, the reformed churches and their leaders reacted in similar ways.

In Germany, Luther's reformation of worship was very conservative. He changed the theology of the mass which set forth the idea of the corporeal presence of Christ in terms of the miracle of transubstantiation effected by the celebrant during the prayer of consecration. In its place he emphasized the necessity of faith on the part of celebrant and people before the sacred bread and wine of the Lord's Supper became consubstantial with the body and blood of Christ. For awhile the Holy Communion in the Lutheran congregations, under Luther's charge, was celebrated in Latin but later was changed to German. He introduced congregational singing into the service and exalted the importance of the sermon, which he called the Sacrament of the Word. He continued such Roman practices as the use of candle and crucifix and pictures. He kept the church year as the basis of Lutheran worship, after deleting the festivals devoted to Mary and the saints.

In Switzerland the Reformation under Zwingli was more radical. He modified the mass to a memorial meal. He exalted the importance of the sermon, as did Luther, but deleted the service of many of its prayers, hymns and much of its music. The services were celebrated in the vernacular and the importance of the calendar of worship minimized.

In Geneva, the Reformation, under John Calvin, was less radical. His service of Holy Communion was based upon the Strasbourg liturgy which was very similar to that of the Lutheran service. He introduced free prayers as well as the fixed prayers, along with congregational singing. Of course, the saints' days and those devoted to Mary were deleted and the festival aspect of the calendar of worship was minimized.

In England, the Reformation, under Henry VIII, consisted largely of the transfer of authority from the pope to the king and parliament. Some of the distinctly Roman Catholic emphases were deleted from the calendar of worship and the services of the church. Eventually, the Book of Common Prayer emerged out of the compromise effected between Protestant and Catholic interests. The basic structure of the Roman calendar was kept with the exception of some of the saints' days and those devoted to Mary. Within the present Anglo-Catholic movement, within the Episcopal Church, many of these days are returning.

Reacting against the established Church of England were the Puritans and the Separatists who wanted lit-

tle of the liturgical calendar of worship. A simple observance of the Lord's Day was enough for them. In
many places, even the two major days of Christmas
and Easter went by unnoticed. Their separation from
Roman Catholic worship was complete and final. Reaction could go no further. No semblance of the old
calendar of worship remained. We must remember,
however, that these Separatists and Puritans always
constituted only a part of Protestant Christianity as a
whole.

Today the major Protestant churches of the world
are in more fundamental agreement regarding the traditional festivals than they have ever been. By and
large, they accept and use the dramatic movement of
the liturgical year which begins with Advent and
closes with the end of Pentecost, according to the Roman calendar, or Trinitytide, according to the Lutheran or Anglican tradition. They use this yearly cycle
of worship to celebrate the birth, life, death and resurrection of Jesus and the birth of the early church. The
heart of the traditional calendar of worship was always
associated with the name of Jesus and, for the most
part, that is the heart of the whole tradition which the
Protestant Church accepts.

Take the Methodist Church, for example. It is the
largest, single Protestant church in the United States.
Furthermore, it has always represented a position mid-
way between such liturgical churches as the Episcopalian and such ultra Protestant churches as the
Congregational. In Methodism's interest in both form
and freedom in worship and in its large number of

adherents, it may be looked upon as a typical Protestant church.

Follow the worship of a Methodist parish church or examine the Book of Worship, published by the official governing body of Methodism. Here you will find the basic skeletal structure of the traditional calendar. Under the title, "Orders of Worship for Occasional Use, Suggested for Festival Observances of the Christian Year," you will find services for Advent, Christmas Sunday, Epiphany, Lent, Good Friday, Easter and Whitsunday. You will also find other services for such days as Thanksgiving. The point to note, however, is the fact that the Methodist Book of Worship reflects the skeletal structure of the old calendar of worship which moves from Advent to Pentecost or Whitsunday.

As another example, take the Book of Worship of the Congregational-Christian churches. It is called the "Book of Worship for Free Churches." There again you will find in section II, orders of worship for the Christian year. There you will find services for the Sundays in Advent, for Christmas, for Epiphany, Lent, Palm Sunday, services for Maundy Thursday, Good Friday, Easter, Whitsunday, Trinity Sunday and All Saints' Day and All Souls' Day. There, in one of the ultra Protestant churches, is a rather complete reflection of the nucleus of the old Roman calendar of worship.

In general, this is the position, too, of the National Council of Churches of Christ in America. In their draft of the Christian year, by Fred Winslow Adams, formerly a member of the Committee on Worship of the Federal Council of Churches, the seven seasons of the Christian year are set forth, six of them taken from the old Roman calendar, namely, Advent, Christmastide, Epiphany, Lent, Eastertide and Whitsuntide. Within this cycle such familiar festivals are included as the Presentation of Jesus in the Temple, The Annunciation, All Saints' Day and All Souls' Day, Ascension Day and the Festival of Christ the King. This really reflects the basic outline of the old church year.

Notice, however, that the traditional Catholic calendar, by no means, has been used in its entirety. The principle of selection has been operative, namely, what is acceptable to Protestants theologically and what is compatible to the Protestant spirit of worship.

Applying these principles, we find that the days devoted to the honor and adoration of Mary are deleted from the Protestant calendar. Though Mary has a warm place in the affections of Protestant Christians, they do not think of her as a member of the Godhead or as a heavenly Being to whom they bring their worship and adoration and intercession. Therefore, all of the worship and festive drama devoted to Mary by the Catholic Church is laid aside by Protestants.

We also find in applying the principle of selection that the days devoted to the honor and worship of the saints have gone. Protestants have been taught to pray directly to God and to offer him their intercessions and their adoration. Again, many of the saints of the church are held in high esteem and in blessed memory by Protestant Christians. These saints are never worshiped, however, or thought of as heavenly Beings to whom prayers and adorations may be directed. It is true that the Episcopal Church is inclined to keep many of these saints' days and to use various prayers and forms of worship appropriate to their observance. We must remember, however, that the Anglican Church is closer in this way to Catholic Christianity than it is to the Protestant movement and that it represents an older tradition at this point.

What Protestantism has done, however, is gradually to accept again the celebration of All Saints' Day on the first of November. Upon this occasion the memory of all the great and loyal Christians is lifted up for thanksgiving, for memory and for instruction. Not only those people whose names have been known for generations are remembered, but also that great multitude of Christians who went their respective and unknown ways trying to do good. In a sermon on "The Communion of Saints," Ernest Fremont Tittle, long time pastor of the First Methodist Church of Evanston, said that All Saints' Day, "might well be observed in every church, emphasizing as it does one of the great affirmations of the Christian faith: I believe in the communion of saints." In this sermon he goes on to define saints as those who had committed themselves to Christ and his church in the hope of becoming better men and women. These are the people whom we remember on this day and this remembrance is being observed more generally.

Thus we see that Protestantism has welcomed the use of the traditional calendar of worship. The early extreme reaction against tradition has been softened by the centuries. Now we recognize tradition as a bond of fellowship that unites the community in Christian sympathy and understanding. It is worth much to know that when the first Sunday of December comes around all the Christians of the community, Catholic and Lutheran, Methodist and Presbyterian, are looking forward with eager longing to the coming of Christmas. How heartening it is to know that friends and neighbors and the whole community celebrate together such great days as Christmas and Ash Wednesday, Good Friday and Easter. In the language of religion, this is known as ecumenical fellowship.

· worship and the common life

Protestant Christians believe in the sanctity of the common life. There is no separation for them between religion and life. In this respect they are the inheritors of the tradition of Israel, set forth in the Old Testament scriptures and the practices of the Jewish community. According to the Old Testament, all life has a certain religious significance. Provision is made for sanctifying the preparation of food, the planting and harvesting of crops, various types of business activities, the affairs of the nation and the crucial moments of a man's life, such as birth, marriage and death. Various rituals for individuals and families and for the community as a whole were developed in elaborate detail in order that the common life might receive religious exaltation.

Protestantism is concerned also that the common life be interpreted in terms of religion and that its dramatic moments be celebrated in the church. Because this is done so frequently and so successfully, men and women feel at home in the familiar round of activity and worship of the church. The concerns which they

encounter at the office and shop, the failures and diffi-
culties which they meet at home, all find reflection in
the worship of the Protestant church. This emphasizes
for them the concern of the church in the total pattern
of their lives.

Protestant Christians believe that unless worship is
tied to the common life, it becomes that kind of a
selfish and romantic venture that makes it the opiate
of the people. Unless the service has an ethical and
practical emphasis the Protestant conscience is disturbed. It remembers the celebrated religious experience of Isaiah when he saw the Lord, high and lifted
up. The Protestant conscience remembers that not only
did Isaiah experience the sublime holiness of God, but
that he also felt the compulsion of God's will upon
him. This compulsion was felt in terms of the social
mission which God wanted Isaiah to undertake, a mission related to the political and international situation
of Israel. Isaiah responded to God's questions, "Whom
shall I send?" and "Who will go for us?" by answer-
ing, "Here am I, send me."

This is the way that Protestant Christians are inclined to feel about the ethical promptings of God
regarding the world in which they live. Finally, worship becomes vital and real for them through the common life and problems of their own day. They do not
want Divine Worship merely to be a celebration of the
memorable events of yesterday, in the archaic idiom of
an olden tongue. If God is to be a living experience in
the every day world, then Sunday morning worship
and the progression of Sunday mornings throughout

the church year must express in the virile language of today the common needs and hopes and experiences that men and women face in the world in which they live.

It is part of the Protestant faith to believe that God does have a word for the whole brilliant mosaic of modern life, from the 12,000 or more books which are published each year to the sleek trains that glide across our prairies, from the problems which farmers face in harvesting their crops and taking them to the warehouses in the city to the bargaining conferences where management and labor sit down together.

God has a word for our world which is at war. It is expressed in the scriptures in the gospel of the Prince of Peace. It is interpreted in the social creeds of the major Protestant churches and in the World Order Days set aside for the consideration of those ways which make for goodwill between the nations and a lasting peace on the earth. It is further interpreted in a good many pulpits, supported by a good many congregations who know that religion is relevant to modern life and has something to say about this matter of war and peace.

God has a word for clean and honest government, as any Christian knows who reads the Old Testament prophets and the Golden Rule of Jesus. Said Isaiah, "Thy princes are rebellious and companions of thieves, every one loveth bribes and followeth after rewards: they judge not the fatherless, neither doth the cause of the widow come unto them." To this word regarding clean government, Protestant congregations respond when special days are set aside for consideration of civic affairs and ministers preach upon these topics. During the winter of 1952, for example, the churches of Chicago were greatly exercised about the reign of terror which gangsterism had fastened upon the political life of the city. A Sunday was set aside when the ministers discussed this situation in their services. Dr. Harrison Ray Anderson of the Fourth Presbyterian Church said in his sermon, "Here in this city, so splendid in many ways, 638 murders have been committed in the last twenty years, of which only thirteen have been solved.

"This fact not only is a condemnation of the administration of the city, but it is an indictment of the citizens of the city and suburbs. Only a lack of moral concern would permit this. The churches of the city must also carry their share of shame."

Other pastors made similar analyses and statements and the following day the Chicago papers carried accounts of the way in which the Sunday pulpits had resounded with the denunciation of citizen apathy that had made possible gangster entrenchment in local politics.

Protestant Christians believe that they have every right and reason to expect such words when they come to church. They want to hear these words, not only in the sermon, but also in the liturgy and in the various days set aside for special worship and consideration of these every day matters. They remember that Jesus worshiped this way, that he pitched his life to the national problems of his own day. The temptation experienced at the beginning of his ministry is a record of the way in which he considered and rejected the three popular solutions of the national problem of his day, namely, the presence of the Roman army of occupation in the midst of Israel. By tying religion to the common life, Jesus lighted the lamp that has illuminated the thinking and worship of Christians ever since those bright historic days.

Thanksgiving Day is a typical example of the way in which the common life has been given religious significance. Every youngster in public school knows the old and interesting story. Because a little group of Separatist Christians, who had come from England, were thankful for their first harvests, they set aside a day for the celebration which included a service of thanksgiving. Since they remembered their utter dependence upon the providence of God to make this harvest possible year after year, they kept the same festival the following autumn. Year after year the Thanksgiving service was held until it became a vital part of the worship of American Christians. It is an example of the way worship gets tied to the common life, in this case, the important matter of an adequate food supply for the year.

Take Brotherhood Day as another example of the way worship is related to the interests and needs of the modern American community. In the average city or town a number of groups live together, racial, religious and social groups that are different from one another. They are dependent upon one another for their well-being and for the vitality of the community. Individual

points of tension arise which often make difficult com-
munication and relationships between these groups. As
an attempt to meet this situation in recent years, the
churches of the community have celebrated Brotherhood Day on the third Sunday in February. Often
Christian ministers and Jewish rabbis exchange pulpits.
Often negro pastors preach to white congregations.
Various devices are used to emphasize the fact that
God has made us all one family. In this way again, the
common life is related to the progression of the church
year.

For some 170 years Protestant Christians have ex-
pected to find in the church the religious recognition
of all civil holidays. If Independence Day fell on a
Sunday and the minister did not recognize it in his
prayers and sermon, the congregation would be
shocked. Protestants expect that when important civil
days appear their religious significance will be set forth
in the service of the parish church. That is why hymns
and prayers, and often anthems, have developed around
the themes of Independence Day, Washington's Birthday, Election Day, Memorial Day, Lincoln's Birthday,
Armistice Day, and other occasions which set forth the
memorable moments of American life. These days all
emerge out of the common life of the community and
very naturally find expression in the worship of the
church.

By now, the fundamental principle of Protestant
worship must be apparent: where the people are, there
is the compassionate concern of the church for their
well-being. Whether men and women are engaged in

commerce or education, in production or management, in artistic creation or in play, the interest of the church surrounds them. There is no aspect of life separate from the concern of religion. Where the people are, there is a point of religious significance and there is material for Divine Worship.

The common life in which the people are involved is relevant to the services of the church. Not only is this common life given expression in the weekly Sunday services where it appears in the prayers and sermon, the readings and the music, it is also set forth in the days of special emphasis. That is why there are found, along with the wonderful pattern of worship that celebrates the appearance and ministry of Jesus, these other days of interest, such as Thanksgiving, the Spring Planting, Election Day, Brotherhood Sunday, and all the other occasions that set forth the common life of the American community.

• the autumn cycle

September marks the beginning of the yearly program of activity in the parish church. The calendar year may start in January and the liturgical year may start in December but anyone who shares in the program planning of the church knows that the actual cycle of festal worship and parish action begins in September. Summer is a natural break in the parish year. When people are back from summer vacations and the school bell calls the youngsters to their studies, the church bell rings its own summons to another year of action.

• back to church

Rally Day always reflects a festive spirit. It is the day that marks the official beginning of the new church year. Planning committees have been at work throughout the summer arranging the program for the coming autumn, winter and spring seasons. When people return from their vacations they expect to swing into the fall round of church activities. The Sunday upon which these activities begin and the day when people appear in their own church to greet one another after summer vacations is called Rally Day.

Rally Day is a good example of the way in which Protestant worship is interpreted in terms of the needs and interests of a particular parish. It is observed on any Sunday following Labor Day to the first or second Sunday in October. The parish chooses a date most convenient to it. The choice is made on the basis of the history of the local church concerning the Sunday that vacationers return and the yearly program can safely begin. This observance has been going on for a long time. No one knows just when it began. Back in 1925 the executive secretary of the International Sunday School Association was asked about the history of the day and said, "I think it is safe to say that the general observance of Rally Day was inaugurated through the International Sunday School Association, possibly following the lead of some of the state conventions."

The observance of Rally Day varies greatly with each local parish. In general, it begins with a Sunday School assembly during the hour set for Church School. All of the departments meet together upon that occasion. For most of the pupils of the Church School this is an unusually interesting experience because during the rest of the year they meet in their separate departments. Now the nave of the church is filled with children, youth and adults. It is a stirring sight to see the entire Church School thus assembled for here are the little youngsters from the nursery department, children in kindergarten, the early grades of school, junior high,

high school and the older youth and adults. Everyone begins to sense something of the spirit of the old hymn, "Like a mighty army moves the Church of God."

Sometimes the Rally Day program is made the occasion for the promotion exercises of the school. Each departmental superintendent will read the list of graduates from his department and present the certificates of promotion to the pupils. As part of this program of graduation often beautiful Bibles are presented to the children who leave the primary department for the junior department. Unusual attention is given to this part of the program for when the child receives his Bible, he has come to a long anticipated moment in his life with the church. During these promotion exercises there is considerable lay participation. The superintendent of the Church School who presides is always a layman. The departmental superintendents are lay people. Perhaps there is a song leader who directs the stirring music of the day. The whole program is characterized by a spirit of eagerness and expectancy, of interesting things to come. At the close of the program in the nave, the pupils go to their new departments for brief periods of organization. The next Sunday they are ready to begin the serious work of the year.

The idea of Rally Day may also be carried through into the church service that day. The minister may use Rally Day as the occasion when he preaches his theme sermon for the year, a sermon whose message will underline the basic purposes and activities during the coming months. Sometimes this fundamental theme of the year will be the result of the intercreative work and planning of the program groups who have met during the summer to outline the year's action. Sometimes this sermon will come from the brooding mind of the pastor who has thought long and deeply about the needs of the parish and who, in a given year, wants to stress some particular needs. On Rally Day often the processional hymn directs the attention of the people to the church to which they are going to give so much of their effort during the coming months. How thrilling it is to meet with old friends again and to rise when the choristers enter the nave singing, "The Church's one foundation is Jesus Christ our Lord."

In many parish churches Rally Day is followed by Religious Education Week. This custom goes back to 1916 when Children's Week was first celebrated by the International Sunday School Association. At that time Maud Baldwin was called to direct the work of the children's division of the Sunday School Association. It seemed to her that all people ought to be reminded from time to time that the realization of their dreams depended upon the religious education of the children of the world. To dramatize this conviction, Maud Baldwin organized the children's workers of the continent for the observance of a Children's Week. During this week every effort was made to point up the fact that childhood is the hope of the world and to show the relationship of religious education to national progress and world happiness. At that time only one out of three of the twenty-five million children in North America, under twelve years of age, was receiving any religious training at all. By dramatizing the program of Christian education and compelling whole communities to face the situation, Maud Baldwin hoped to vitalize Christian work among children and youth.

Through the years many forms of action were devised for Children's Week, which later was changed to Religious Education Week, and moved from spring to autumn. Sermons were preached, parents' meetings were held in which the work of the Church School was explained, exhibits were put in store windows down town, visits were made to the homes of the children and sometimes a parade with floats was held to set forth all the work of the Church School. Pageants and plays were given in the town hall, a children's festival of song and story was often held and other means devised to challenge the interest of people in childhood. This week, with its emphasis upon the educational program of the church, is one means that Protestantism uses to capture the attention of its lay people to the task which they must perform if religion is going to live.

· that they all may be one

During the last ten years almost all the parish churches associated with the National Council of Churches of Christ in America have shared in the worldwide celebration of Holy Communion on the first Sunday in October. In doing this, they have tried to provide an answer to that hope expressed in Jesus' high priestly prayer, "that they all may be one; as thou, Father, art in me, and I in thee, that they also may be one in us: that the world may believe that thou hast sent me." In celebrating Holy Communion simultaneously on the first Sunday in October, Protestant churches give evidence of the new spirit of fellowship which characterizes modern Protestantism. Even though the community is confronted with the division of Christians into a number of denominations, such as Methodist, Presbyterian and Lutheran, these denominations no longer mean fundamental divisiveness. Today there is a sense of mutual respect, understanding and needs among the churches. Because there is also a sense of opportunity in a united Christendom, these churches are engaged together in many enterprises for the good of the community. From time to time, various services are held which express the mutual interest of churches in one another and register their fundamental unity.

Holy Communion was chosen as the one service which all churches have in common. Roman Catholic and Eastern Orthodox, Congregational and Baptist, Lutheran, Episcopalian and Presbyterian, and all the other branches of Christendom celebrate the Lord's Supper. The Roman Catholics call it the Mass, the Eastern Orthodox speak of the Divine Liturgy, the Anglicans often call it the Eucharist, and the Baptists speak of it as the Lord's Supper and the Methodists call it the Holy Communion. Fundamentally, it is the same service for whenever bread and wine are consecrated and consumed, there is the sacred sacramental meal of the Christian church. Because all the churches have this particular sacramental service in common, it

· 42

was chosen for simultaneous use on the first Sunday in October. This day has now come to be known as World Communion Sunday. It is one of the important contributions of Protestantism to the Christian calendar of worship.

On that day a special effort is made to invite all the members of all parish churches to attend the Sunday service. Very helpful materials are published by the National Council of Churches to attract the interest of the more than thirty-five million people making up the national membership of its constituent churches. Then each parish church celebrates Holy Communion according to its own rite. In the Episcopal Church and Methodist Church this will often be a rather elaborate choral celebration with candles and flowers, with ceremonial and beautiful liturgy, much of which goes back to ancient sources. In other churches, like the Baptist Church, this service will be very simple, with a minimum of ritual and ceremony. In all cases, however, congregations have a sense of their solidarity with other congregations and their membership together in that transcendant church that the creeds call, "The Body of Christ," or, "The Communion of Saints."

Another expression of inter-church fellowship on World Communion Sunday is the custom of having an ecumenical service that evening. An ecumenical service is a new kind of union service. Members of various churches will meet together upon this occasion to share in exercises of worship that have been taken from their respective liturgies. Each participating church and pastor thus make a contribution to the ecumenical

liturgy in use that evening. Thus Protestant Christians
come to feel at home together as they share in the
liturgical usages of their respective churches.

A typical ecumenical service may proceed in some
such manner as this:

> Processional Hymn—The Church's one
> foundation
> A Call to Worship or A Responsive Act
> of Adoration
> The Gloria Patri
> Greetings and a declaration of fellow-
> ship—by the president of the local
> Council of Churches
> The Old Testament Lesson
> The Anthem
> The New Testament Lesson
> The Fellowship of Prayer
> For the Nation
> For World Brotherhood
> For the Church
> The Lord's Prayer in many tongues
> (pastors, representing various foreign
> language groups in the community, will
> rise to repeat this common prayer in
> their respective languages)
> A Hymn of Fellowship
> The Sermon
> The Offering and its Presentation
> Closing Prayer and Benediction
> A Hymn of Triumph

These ecumenical services have become increasingly popular in recent years. The local pastors take pride in their participation in the service. The whole community looks forward to the visiting preachers who are often invited to give the sermon. Generally, these are nationally known men who publish the great journals of religion, who lead the important committees of the National Council of Churches, who head up the work of the great denominations or who have the pastoral care of the great churches of the country. In the autumnal calendar of worship, these services are triumphant festal moments with colorful processions, stirring messages and a wonderful sense of togetherness.

· reformation

On October 31, 1517, Martin Luther nailed his famous ninety-five theses to the chapel door of the Castle Church at Wittenberg. Each blow of the hammer broke a link in the chain that had fastened all Christians of Western Europe to the Roman Catholic Church. To that act, we may date the opening movement of the Protestant Reformation. The Reformation was the crisis in the history of the church. The unity of Christendom had been broken 500 years before in the great schism between East and West. At that time the metropolitan sees of Rome and Constantinople severed their diplomatic and ecclesiastical relationships. Eastern Orthodoxy went its way and Roman Catholicism went its way. Now the complacency of Western European Christianity was broken again by Martin

Luther's hammer. The church of Western Europe, which had functioned almost like a unanimous being, was broken into many divisions. Under Luther in Germany, the Lutheran movement resulted from this religious revolution. In Zurich, under Zwingli, the Reformed Church movement began. In Geneva, under Calvin, the Calvinist and Presbyterian movements were formed. Meanwhile, other Protestant groups arose, such as the Anabaptists in Germany and the low countries, the Episcopalians in England and the Presbyterians in Scotland. The Protestant Reformation was in full swing.

The emerging churches had taken a decisive position. They rested their case on the freedom of the human spirit. They believed in a man's right to think for himself concerning religion. They believed that the informed mind and a sensitive conscience needed no authoritative church to impose a pattern of religious thought and action upon it. Each Protestant Christian, assuming his fundamental sincerity, had the right to think for himself and to form his own design for religious living, based upon his own encounter with God.

Out of that movement emerged the political tradition of democracy as we know it. Where Protestantism developed most vigorously, there the institution of democracy presently emerged. Human freedom came to fine expression in Switzerland and England, in Scotland, in Norway and Sweden, and, of course, in the United States of America. These are all predominately Protestant countries for political freedom and religious freedom go hand in hand.

No wonder that Reformation has a festival of its own. Increasing numbers of churches are celebrating the Festival of the Reformation on the Sunday nearest to October 31. These festival services are often held within the individual parish. The altar and pulpit appointments are changed to red, the color of Reformation. The great hymns are sung, such as Martin Luther's hymn, "A mighty fortress is our God, a bulwark never failing." Sermons are preached which reflect the spirit of Reformation and which point out the continuing need for vigilance lest our hard won liberties gradually be lost. Sometimes community services of this nature are held on Reformation Sunday. Often the various synodical groups of the Lutheran churches will rent the largest auditorium in town and go there with colorful processions and church banners, with massed choirs and stirring preachers. In some communities the local Council of Churches will arrange similar services which dramatize for the entire community the inestimable gift of freedom which Protestant Christianity has given to the world.

• some november festivals

One of the best loved days of the church year is All Saints' Day. Its traditional date is November 1. It is the moment when the church lifts into memory and thanksgiving all the great and gifted saints who have adorned its life through the centuries. Great names come to mind upon that occasion: Peter, James and John, Stephen, Paul and Barnabas and other saints of the New Testament; Clement, the theologian of Alexandria, Jerome who translated the Bible into Latin, Augustine who shaped the thought of the church for centuries, Francis of Assissi who brought a new spirit of loving kindness and simple beauty to religion, Luther and the Protestant Reformation, and all the other golden names that star the pages of church history.

All Saints' Day is followed on November 2 by All Souls' Day. That is the occasion when we remember the great multitude of good and conscientious people who have sought to live according to their Christian understanding and who have made this world a happier place for other people. Their names are unknown and their lives have been unsung, except by their immediate friends, but life itself would be the poorer if they had never lived. On All Souls' Day we delight to remember the fact that it takes the hard work and the loving kindness of multitudes of people through all the generations to keep this world as good as it is.

Part of the Protestant Church never gave up the observance of these days. In the Anglican Church, for example, All Saints' Day was dearly loved through the years. Many an Episcopalian remembers either the cathedral or the parish church celebration of that day. Now it is being used again by many of the Protestant churches in connection with All Souls' Day on the Sunday nearest to November 1. It is the occasion when we set forth in memory and thanksgiving the lives of Christian saints, known and unknown, who have supported the work of the church and filled the world

with loving kindness. One inevitable hymn begins the
All Saints' Day service:

.   "For all the saints, who from their labors
rest,
Who Thee by faith before the world con-
fessed,
Thy name, O Jesus, be forever blessed,
Alleluia! Alleluia!

From earth's wide bounds, from ocean's
farthest coast,
Through gates of pearl streams in the
countless host,
Singing to Father, Son, and Holy Ghost,
Alleluia! Alleluia!

Conceivably, each congregation might hear that
Sunday a sermon setting forth the meaning of this
day, a sermon like that delivered by Ernest Fremont
Tittle to the congregation of the First Methodist
Church of Evanston in which he said:

"The 'communion of saints,' beginning in the local
church and congregation, reaches out toward the ends
of the earth. Nor does it stop even there. Uniting the
living in some real way with the dead, it reaches to
a world unseen and eternal. The early Christians spoke
of their dead as 'those who have gone before,' and they
remembered before God those of their number who
had gone before and dared to believe that these de-
parted ones held them in memory and helped them
by their prayers and intercessions to God. This may

seem strange to us, this idea of a 'communion of saints' that overpasses not only distance but even death. We may shrink from it, perhaps, as something alien to Protestant belief and practice. But first let it be noted that what is here in question is prayer for the saints and not prayer to the saints, which is another matter. And further let it be noted that prayer for those who have gone before is surely in keeping with the Christian faith that when a man dies that is not the end of him.

"If we are convinced that Christianity is true, why should we not pray for those of our number who have gone before and especially for those we have known and loved, for whom often we prayed when they were with us in the flesh? And why should we hesitate to believe that those who in their days on earth knew and loved us still hold us in memory and help us by their prayers and intercessions to God? This, of course, is an incredible belief for anyone who feels bound to reject the Christian faith about life after death. But what if you are convinced that Christianity is true?"

Another November festival is World Peace Sunday. It falls on the Sunday nearest to Armistice Day, November 11. Its observance is another major contribution of the Protestant Church to the calendar of worship for the Protestant emphasis in Christianity always seeks to relate religion to the great issues and major problems of the day.

What universal appeal World Peace Sunday has for mankind! All over the world men and women lift up their hands and their voices to God in the cry for peace. They are tired of sending their sons to war. They are broken with the anxieties and hardships of continuous conflict. They are utterly discouraged over the need for spending so much time in the fruitless labor of paying for the awful economic destruction of war in the past. Deeply they long for peace and in many a prayer of petition and intercession set forth their need. How natural, therefore, that the church set aside a Sunday in which this longing of mankind may come to liturgical expression and to fulfillment in the service.

Consider a typical service on World Peace Sunday, one from the calendar of worship at the First Methodist Church of Racine, Wisconsin. Upon one such occasion, the service began with the very thrilling hymn, in which the organ trumpets set forth the theme:

·   "God of our fathers, whose almighty hand
         Leads forth in beauty all the starry
         band."

It continued with an anthem by Henry Hallstrom written in modern music idiom, "For the Peace of the World," which concludes with the words, "We pray thee that all men of all lands shall be good neighbors and dwell together in thy peace and in thy love." The gospel for the day set forth the commandment, "Render unto Caesar the things that are Caesar's, but unto God the things that are God's." The minister preached on the topic: Strategy for Peace. He stated his theme in the opening paragraph of the sermon, "To live or not to live is the crucial problem of our day. That old question that disturbed the mind of Hamlet is now disturbing the mind of the whole world.

"To live or not to live is a question which implies that man has the ability to make a decision, to cast a ballot in favor of life or death. Such a decision now confronts the nations of the world. To live by means of a strategy designed to secure world peace or to die by means of international selfishness and confusion that will set off the atomic bombs of the world, that is the decision which now we must make."

He went on to suggest the need for strategy in peace making, that we take account of the moral laws inherent in the nature of God, laws which when obeyed secure the support of the universe for those things which make for life. Such strategy calls for the development of a peace point of view that will influence the public opinion of the world. This calls for a coalition of all the peace forces of every major social organization in existence. Such a public opinion and coalition is decisive in political action. The sermon concluded with a call for the support of the use of the United Nations as an instrument designed to maintain the peace.

Thanksgiving Day is another typical Protestant festival in November. It goes back to the Plymouth colony when Governor Bradford set apart a day for thanksgiving in 1621 in order to thank God for the harvest of the year. Ever since that early colonial day Protestant churches have observed this feast. In recent years the day has been marked by community services. Either on the eve of Thanksgiving or the morning of the feast people gather together in one of the churches of the community for a union service consisting of hymns and anthems of praise and thanksgiving, prayers and litanies of adoration to God and a sermon preached by one of the pastors recounting the social basis for thanksgiving that year. You will be interested in reading the full account of this old custom as set forth by Ralph and Adelin Linton in their story of Thanksgiving, entitled, "We Gather Together."

· advent

Autumn moves inevitably to that reflective spirit preceding Christmas that we call Advent. It is a season of hope; it is a time when we remember that just at the point of man's despair God gives man courage with the promise of a great gift. Through a long history of adversity the Hebrew people found that man cannot make a go of life alone. When an individual or group becomes badly beaten up, which misfortune happened to the Hebrew people repeatedly, they know that only God can sustain them. This prompted the Hebrew people to look for a divine Savior to help them. Living in an impossible geographic situation, with world powers surrounding them on every hand, these people knew that only through the grace and the help of God, who might conceivably send a Savior, could they come through alive.

That Advent hope the Church remembers every year. It unites its own hopes and fears and aspirations with those of these ancient people to wait again for the wonderful moment when the Savior is born once more into the hearts and minds of men. This hope is simply

a remembrance of the basic fact that in meeting diffi-
culty one ought always to look for the help of God.
It is a reminder of the fact that a wise and compassionate God, and Father of our Lord Jesus Christ, will
give a man help and security and courage. It is the
assurance that in his hour of sharpest need, Almighty
God, through Jesus Christ, is coming soon to help him.

Advent worship is characterized by the spirit of expectancy. Services point to the coming of Christmas.
Worshipers coming to the nave for the first Sunday
in Advent find that the altar and pulpit appointments
have been changed to purple, the color of somber reflection. The Advent spirit of expectancy emerges out
of the sober reflection of the mind upon the world's
great need of a Savior. Sermons analyze the social situation and point out the need for such ethical ideals as
set forth by Jesus if the problems of the day are to be
solved. Hymns are sung which look forward to the
advent of Jesus. A typical hymn of this nature is the
one by Charles Wesley:

> "Come, Thou long expected Jesus,
> Born to set Thy people free,
> From our fears and sins release us;
> Let us find our rest in Thee.
> Israel's Strength and Consolation,
> Hope of all the earth Thou art;
> Dear Desire of every nation,
> Joy of every longing heart."

Prophetic lessons are read from the Bible in which
the prophets of the Old Testament set forth the great

hope of Israel, as Isaiah did when he said, "And there shall come forth a rod out of the stem of Jesse, and a Branch shall grow out of his roots. And the spirit of the Lord shall rest upon him, the spirit of wisdom and understanding, the spirit of counsel and might, the spirit of knowledge and of the fear of the Lord . . . And in that day there shall be a root of Jesse, which shall stand for an ensign of the people; to it shall the Gentiles seek: and his rest shall be glorious."

The second Sunday in December, which is usually the second Sunday in Advent, is known as Universal Bible Sunday. All over the Protestant world this Sunday is used for the recognition of the fundamental importance of the Bible in the Christian religion. The American Bible Society sends to all of the churches materials which each year emphasize some particular phase of the Bible in Christian living. These materials include responsive readings and prayers, sermon suggestions, hymns and other materials which will be used simultaneously by the Protestant Christian world on that particular Sunday.

This is another distinctive Protestant festival which stems from the Reformation interest in the Bible. It was Martin Luther's conviction, shared by the other Protestant reformers, that the Bible must be translated into the vernacular and be made available to every home. The reformers wanted their people to read the Bible. They knew that it contained the words of life. It was their belief that when men and women studied the Bible they understood the truths of religion more thoroughly and became better Christians. No wonder that Protestant Christians should perpetuate this interest in Bible reading by devoting at least one Sunday to a recognition of its importance.

The spirit of Universal Bible Sunday is set forth in the collect for the day in Common Prayer: "Blessed Lord, who hast caused all holy Scriptures to be written for our learning; Grant that we may in such wise hear them, read, mark, learn, and inwardly digest them, that by patience and comfort of thy holy Word, we may embrace, and ever hold fast, the blessed hope of everlasting life, which thou hast given us in our Savior Jesus Christ. Amen."

· christmas

There has developed around the celebration of Christmas the most brilliant and charming mosaic of services and customs to be found in the entire calendar of worship. When John closed the Fourth Gospel, he wrote, "And there are also many other things which Jesus did, the which, if they should be written every one, I suppose that even the world itself could not contain the books that should be written." This magnificent exaggeration has nearly come true concerning the celebration of the Holy Nativity.

Christmas has always been a festival beloved by the Protestant Church. Tradition takes us back to Martin Luther and his own love of the German folk customs concerning Christmastide. One tradition persists that he introduced the familiar Christmas tree, lighted with candles, and that from Germany the glittering tree spread to other parts of Christendom.

It is true that for awhile, among some of the Separatist and Puritan groups, the celebration of Christmas was denied. Parliament of 1644 forbade some of the merry making which went on at Christmas time in England and we know that in our own New England its celebration was also frowned upon. In fact, the keeping of Christmas and All Saints' Day, not to mention the making of mince pies, was actually forbidden by the Blue Laws of the Massachusetts and the New Hampshire colonies. As was suggested before, however, these groups represented but a small segment of the Protestant world. The Lutherans and Anglicans always enjoyed Christmastide. Since the intensity of Puritanism waned, the rest of the Protestant world has enjoyed this First Festival of the Deity.

Many customs have adorned this festal season. For years, in the freer Protestant churches, many of the Christmas festivities centered in the Sunday School program which gave parents and children an opportunity to have Christmas together at the church. Occasionally, city parishes and many a rural church still use the Sunday School program. It is composed of congregational singing, of recitations by the children with an occasional dramatic skit or pantomime setting forth the Christmas theme. Just as yesterday, Santa Claus still comes today in some of these churches to close the Sunday School program. He carries a big sack over his shoulder and distributes the little cartons of candy and other gifts to the children.

Gradually, however, a different type of program replaced this miscellaneous program of the Sunday School. Many Church Schools began to organize a White Gift Christmas or a children's choral service or a nativity pageant of some kind. For many years the White Gift Christmas was very popular and it is still used the world around. It was first used by a Methodist Church in Painsville, Ohio back in 1904 and was based upon the old legend of Cathay which told about the white feast and gifts of love on the great King's birthday. It helped to bring back the real significance of this Festival of the Holy Nativity to Protestant Sunday Schools that had gone overboard in the matter of holiday entertainment. Careful preparation was made ahead of time in the matter of giving at Christmastime. The service of White Gifts For the King is not to be arranged lightly and without preparation. Gifts of self are brought, of service and of substance. Individual pupils were encouraged to write on cards certain commitments which they would make as a gift to Christ the King. These commitments might be matters of character development and personality change. They might be matters of different forms of personal service that were to be rendered during the coming months. Children, youth and adults took great pleasure in making genuine commitments of this nature and many a church grew and many a community became better because of the white gifts that were made to the King at Christmastime. Group gifts in terms of money and materials were often made. All of these gifts were brought to the foot of a white cross in a white chancel at the Christmas service developed around this theme.

Other churches produced Christmas plays, pageants and operettas as a more significant way of setting forth the Christmas theme. For many years both the play and the operetta, "Why the Chimes Rang" was very popular. This presentation was based upon the story written by Raymond Alden. Anyone who has heard that simple and charming story will never forget the beauty of the gifts made by the little boy to the Savior, gifts which set the chimes in the church tower ringing. In recent years, the public school has absorbed so much of the time and energy of Protestant children that there is no longer the interest in these Christmas programs and dramatic presentations that characterized a former time. Much has been lost as a result. Today the public school demands endless rehearsals during the Advent season for a gigantic Christmas concert and pageant and, in a sense, rushes the season and takes the pleasure out of a more simple program in the parish church.

Nevertheless, Christmas continues to be a very rich season in Protestant churches. The smaller children have their various departmental parties during the holidays when they invite their parents and present a very simple, informal program, play group games, receive gifts and finish off with the inevitable Christmas food. The older youth have their holiday parties. Sometimes they are vary swank affairs. This social life and merry making during the Christmas season is not confined to the children and youth, however. Many a church has a big holiday party. This may take the form of an Old English dinner, presided over by the lord and lady of the manor and presenting the kind of a program and feast that might have occurred in an old baronial hall. It may take the form of a Swedish smorgasbord when tables are heaped with good things to eat and the church family gathers together for happy fellowship.

More and more, however, the distinctive opportunities for Christmas worship are being used by the Protestant Church. Three forms of worship are of particular interest in the celebration of the Holy Nativity. For many years the Episcopalian Church has celebrated a midnight service of Holy Communion. The church and the chancel are beautifully decorated with Christmas greens, with roses and poinsettias and other festival flowers. Often the entire church is illuminated with hundreds of flickering candles. Familiar Christmas hymns and carols are sung and Holy Communion is celebrated to the accompaniment of some great choral setting such as Gounod's "St. Cecelia's Mass." An increasing number of other churches, such as the Methodist, are now using Christmas Eve for a similar service of Holy Communion. Parishioners gather in the softly lighted church to sing the beautiful old hymns, to hear the first lessons of Christmas read and to read the liturgy of the Lord's Supper, parts of which are sung by the choir in one of the fine musical settings for Holy Communion. Then the bread and wine are consecrated upon the altar and the people come down to the chancel rail to receive these sacred symbols of the presence of Christ in the church. Many

Protestants find that this is a very satisfying way in which to recognize the Holy Nativity.

Another type of service is a choral service or a musical service. Often this is held at 11:00 o'clock on Christmas Eve. Churches are decorated with the traditional Christmas flowers and vestments. Clergy and choir appear in the chancel to lead the congregation in the singing of hymns and carols and the reading of Christmas litanies and prayers. Sometimes the choir will sing a Christmas cantata or will present a miscellaneous group of Christmas anthems. To the accompaniment of this beautiful music, the congregation welcomes the new born child.

Every parish church celebrates Christmas at the Sunday morning service preceding the festal day itself. Again the Christmas music is sung, some of the Christmas lessons are read and the pastor preaches a sermon which discusses the significance of Christ's birth in terms of the needs of people alive today. In these ways and in other ways, too, the event which changed the course of history and divided the centuries into the years before Christ, and the years anno Domini is brought into the church for celebration during Divine Worship.

See what several churches do for their Christmastide observance. There is Old South Church in Boston, one of the memorable bastions of New England Protestantism. It stands on Copley Square, near Trinity Church, and has long been a familiar landmark in Boston. Listed on the calendar of their Christmas program for one particular year was the following schedule of activities: On the fourth Sunday in Advent, which was the Sunday preceding Christmas, Morning Worship was devoted to the Christmas theme. A preludial organ recital included some well loved Christmas organ music, such as "In dulci jubilo" by Marcel Dupré. The service began with the hymn, "Hark the herald angels sing," and moved through the familiar Christmas lessons and choral festival music and the sermon by Dr. Meek on the topic: The News and the Good News. The service concluded with everyone standing for the "Hallelujah Chorus."

On Christmas Eve Old South Church celebrated with a candlelight service consisting of congregational singing of Christmas hymns, a number of carols by the choir, and the reading of an original Christmas story, entitled, "Having Eyes, They See Not," by Dr. Meek. Other events on the holiday program included Christmas caroling and Christmas parties with a Watch Night service held in the chapel on New Year's Eve.

Take a train a thousand miles west to Evanston, Illinois, the seat of Northwestern University, and celebrate Christmas with the First Methodist Church. That parish has a well-defined holiday schedule which always includes a very wonderful presentation in the nave of the church of the Nativity in Scripture, pantomime and song. This is produced by the Church School and the various choirs of the church. It begins with the opening exercises of worship, such as hymn and prayer, and then a series of pantomimes according to the manner of familiar paintings which set forth the events of the Nativity. Associated with all pantomimes are the interpretive readings of the pastor, who reads from the rear balcony of the church, and the singing of appropriate carols by the soloists and choirs of the church.

These pictorial groups in the chancel, in exquisite costuming, set forth the prophecy, the annunciation, the apparition of the shepherds, the wise men before Herod, the adoration of the shepherds, and the wise men before the sacred crib, and the processional of light which is composed of innumerable children and youth of the Church School, moving down the center aisle of the darkened church with electric tapers held high in their hands, to group around the crib in the chancel for the final pantomime, the prophecy fulfilled. This Nativity pageant has been presented by the First Methodist Church of Evanston for many years and is one of the contributions of Protestant worship to the beauty and art and wonder of Christmastime.

In the calendar of this church the Sunday morning service, preceding Christmas Day, is always devoted to the Christmas theme. It includes Christmas hymns, great anthems sung by their superb choir, and a Christmas sermon in which the pastor sets forth the social implications of Christmastime in no uncertain way. Through the years, these sermons have discussed such themes as "From Bethlehem to Bikini," "The Wonder of Jesus," "Jesus After Nineteen Centuries," "The Savior of the World," "Christmas Morning," and "The Light of the World Still Shines." Still another event on the Christmas calendar of this church is a midnight Christmas Eve service of sacred music. The carillon in the tower announces the Christmas theme with a preludial recital. Singing from the fountain foyer, before entering the sanctuary, is the chancel choir in a group of carols. Then the great Christmas processional opens the service, which moves from choral prayers and responsive readings to selections from a Christmas cantata or oratorio, and to the final benediction after midnight. Candles illuminate the church, flowers adorn the altars and worshipers are sure that in the beauty of this service the very gates of heaven stand ajar.

On the social calendar of this church is a holiday party sometime during the Christmas season. This is a festal occasion when the members of the church sit down for a great holiday dinner, for entertainment of various kinds and for good fellowship together. Meanwhile, various departments of the Church School have their own Christmas services and parties, thus combining to make Christmastide one of the bright spots of the year.

Many Protestant churches conclude the Christmas season with some kind of a service on New Year's Eve. Often this service is combined with a party or some social activities. The parish will meet perhaps for dinner, at 8:00 o'clock, will enjoy games and fellowship and sometimes listen to a program or concert. Then at 11:00 o'clock the congregation will adjourn to the nave of the church for a solemn New Year's Eve service. Often this will take the form of Holy Communion. At other times the pastor will preach a New Year's Eve sermon and people may make vows and commitments regarding the New Year.

# the autumn cycle

Both the Congregational and Christian Book of Worship and the Methodist Book of Worship contain services for the use of churches on New Year's Eve. In the Congregational service an extended act of confession is outlined, it being the thought that New Year's Eve is a good time to put aside the sins which beset one during the past year, thus being in a position to face the New Year with a clean slate. The Methodist service is a modern adaptation of the old Covenant Service as used by John Wesley at the French church at Spitalfields on August 11, 1755. John Wesley issued that service in pamphlet form which was used without alteration for many years. His brother, Charles, wrote a special covenant hymn which is still part of the service:

> "Come let us use the grace divine,
> And all with one accord,
> In a perpetual covenant join
> Ourselves to Christ the Lord."

The service calls attention to the need for repeated renewal of one's Christian vows of consecration. After certain acts of adoration and thanksgiving and confession, the people called Methodists then make their covenant, which begins with the words, "and now, beloved, let us bind ourselves with willing bonds to our covenant God, and take the yoke of Christ upon us.

"This taking of his yoke upon us means that we are heartily content that he appoint us our place and work and that he alone be our reward."

The service concludes with the covenant prayer, be-

gun by the minister, continued by the people and concluding with the words, "And now, O glorious and
blessed God, Father, Son and Holy Spirit, thou art
mine, and I am thine. So be it. And the covenant which
I have made on earth, let it be ratified in heaven.
Amen."

The General Commission on Evangelism of the
Methodist Church has published an additional Office
of Worship for New Year's Eve, to be used by an
individual in his solitude, by families and groups of
friends, by the youth groups waiting for the New Year
or by a congregation at a Watch Night Service. This
Office of Worship begins with an act of remembrance:

"Lovely was this Christmas season . . . Bravely we
gathered the traditions of many years with which to
greet the Christ on his Nativity. Though the world
was bathed in pain and despair, all the blessed dead
of many generations and our loved ones far away in
lonely or in dangerous places would have us keep this
ancient feast in order that civilization itself may be
kept alive. Old fires were lighted and Christmas tapers
were burned and beautiful faces of far away and yesterday shone upon us in the silvered light of memory . . .
The ancient peaceful stars looked down as always upon
this troubled earth. From cloud banks high in the
heavens, choristers declared again:

> Lift up. . . lift up. . . . lift up your
> hearts.
> Glory to God . . . glory to God. . . .
> glory to God in the highest,

and on earth peace, good will toward
men."

From the act of remembrance the service moves to
a consideration of the voice of God in which the individual and the group meditate upon the duties and the
opportunities of the New Year. It concludes with a
consideration of the voice of the New Year in terms
of prayers of petition and an act of dedication to God
through all the New Year. When the benediction is
pronounced and the final hymn of assurance sung, the
New Year is welcomed and the autumnal cycle of
festival days is brought to a close.

Almighty God,

who didst make Thyself known to mankind through the holy nativity of Jesus Christ our Lord, we adore Thee on this Christmas Sunday.

We rejoice in all the Christmas stories that reflect the joy of mankind in that starlit night peopled with angels from the inaccessible lights and filled with their choral music that announced the birth of the long desired One. We remember again that simple sanctuary in a Bethlehem stable which had been glorified by the Mother and Child, the anxious father and the adoring shepherds. Today we again become part of this wondrous moment that divided the centuries and changed the thinking of mankind and turned the hearts of people to Thee. Along with all the multitudes who praise Thee for that moment of promise and benediction, we also sing,

"O come let us adore Him,
Christ the Lord."

For good deeds that are prompted by the world's memory of Jesus, for generous gifts that are given and lives that are brought to Thee by the meaning of these festal days, we adore Thee, blessed God.

For the seed germ of a world-wide peace that shall be beautiful upon this earth, for those designs for living based upon goodwill and loving kindness, upon justice and cooperation among people and nations, for this faith that Jesus prompted in the possibility of peace in any generation, we thank Thee, O living God.

For the beauty of Christmas customs that adorn the days of the year, that touch the heart and bring to mind again the dear and lovely faces of the long ago to shine upon us in the silvered candlelight—for all of these gifts and for the simple sense of the living Presence of Christ, we adore Thee on this holy festival; through Jesus Christ our Lord.

Amen.

·   **the winter cycle**

Winter has its own rhythm and cycle of interest in the Protestant Church. After the exhilarating events of autumn, January is a quiet month. People can neither work nor worship at concert pitch all the time. There are rhythms in the soul's relation to God just as there are in other areas of a man's life. Often this spiritual rhythm coincides with the rhythm of nature. Periods of jubilant pageantry in worship are followed by days of quiet reflection. Winter is such a time.

Often in the southland, where church attendance is accelerated during the winter months, there is a natural break in activities after Christmastide is past. In the north, particularly in rural areas, church attendance drops and activities are reduced for a few weeks during the bitter January weather. One young pastor, who had been sent from the city to a northern rural church, was astonished out of his judgment by the January rebound of the calendar of worship. During the autumn his church had been largely attended but, to his utter amazement, after New Year's Day, less than two dozen people appeared for Sunday Morning Worship. He was so astonished that he announced the hymn, "Onward Christian Soldiers," and asked the people to follow him in a march around the church. As part of the procession, he led them across the chancel platform. After they had returned to their pews, he made public inquiry, "How do you like the appearance of an empty church from the pulpit?" He had not realized that in this rural northern area attendance takes that kind of a winter slump.

It is still as true now as it was at the close of the 16th century:

•
> "When icicles hang by the wall
>   And Dick the shepherd blows his nail,
> And Tom bears logs into the hall,
>   And milk comes frozen home in pail;
> When blood is nipt, and ways be foul,
> Then nightly sings the staring owl
>   Tuwhoo!"

• january

The first festival of the winter cycle is that of the Epiphany. It comes upon January 6. Originally it was an Eastern festival, associated both with the baptism of Jesus and his nativity. In the West, when December 25 was chosen as the date for Christmas, the Epiphany was celebrated in memory of the Magi who came to visit the young Christ Child. This is part of the Christmas story told by the author of the first

Gospel. It begins with the familiar words, "Now when Jesus was born in Bethlehem of Judaea in the days of Herod the king, behold, there came wise men from the east to Jerusalem. Saying, Where is he that is born King of the Jews? for we have seen his star in the east, and are come to worship him . . ."

Western practice, from which the Protestant calendar of worship is derived, celebrates Epiphany in the spirit of this story. The word Epiphany means manifestation. The Epiphany describes the manifestation of Jesus to the Magi who traditionally represented the nations of the world. It sets forth the fact that Jesus had come as a Savior, not only to his own people, but also to mankind. Tradition delights to picture these Magi representing China, India and Ethiopia as symbolic of the entire world to which the Savior had come.

The spirit of the day is characterized in the old Anglican collect of Common Prayer: "O God, who by the leading of a star didst manifest thy only-begotten Son to the Gentiles; Mercifully grant that we, who know thee now by faith, may after this life have the fruition of thy glorious Godhead; through Jesus Christ our Lord. Amen."

In our Protestant churches Epiphany is usually celebrated on the Sunday nearest to January 6. Christmas decorations are still in place: great green wreaths between the windows of the nave, the altar and pulpit adorned with their festival coverings of white and gold, festoons of cedar and pine giving the Christmastide atmosphere to the chancel and the festival colors and lights of the church making an appropriate setting for the reading of the last of these Christmas lessons which tell about the visit of the wise men to the Nativity crib. Such hymns are sung as:

· "Brightest and best of the sons of the morning,
Dawn on our darkness and lend us Thine aid;
Star of the East, the horizons adorning,
Guide where our infant Redeemer is laid."

For his sermon that day, the minister may preach on the general topic of the meaning of Christ for the world. The general theme of the Epiphany festival is the relation of Jesus to the world: the way in which his insights may illumine our darkened times; the way in which his spirit of love may bring the nations of the world together; the way in which his devotion to the Kingdom of God may bring to pass the beloved community upon the earth.

One of the great Protestant services celebrating the Epiphany is that held each year by Chicago University in Rockefeller Chapel. Worshipers enter this great Gothic chapel, the mosaic ceiling of which and the distant altar at the end of the far apse can hardly be seen at night. As they await the beginning of the service, presently the organ begins Bach's old choral prelude, "Von Himmel hoch da komm' ich her." Cantor and organ announce the familiar theme of the service in the old Scriptural words, "In the beginning was the Word, and the Word was with God, and the

the winter cycle

Word was God. In him was life; and the life was the light of men." Gently and beautifully, almost imperceptibly, the a cappella choir, singing from the far off balcony in the rear of the nave, begins the old Appalachian carol, "Jesus the Christ is Born." Then we look toward the lectern where the celebrant reads the Gospels from St. John and St. Luke which are followed by the response, "Hosanna in excelsist." Again, singing from the rear balcony, other carols fill the nave. Then the office lesson is read from St. Matthew. Again "Hosanna in excelsist" breaks forth from the choir and more carols are sung, including the charming "Lo, how a Rose e'er Blooming" and Praetorius'

> "Through the night as all the world slept,
>   Alleluia!
> Christ His lonely vigil in the manger
>   kept."

The organ prelude picks up the Praetorius theme and the processional hymn begins. The choir, having sung from the balcony, now moves down the center aisle of the nave while the congregation unites with them in singing:

> "As with gladness men of old
> Did the guiding star behold."

The offering is then received for the support of the University Settlement while the choir, now in the chancel, sings several Bach chorales. After the offering has been received and presented at the altar, the celebrant reads the office sentences, "Ye are the light of

· 73

the world. A city that is set on a hill cannot be hid. Neither do men light a candle, and put it under a bushel, but on a candlestick; and it giveth light unto all that are in the house." During the reading of these sentences, the acolytes bring their tapers to the altar candles and light them. Then the lesson from Matthew 10 is read in which Jesus commissions his disciples to go out into the cities and countryside to take the light of his gospel. While these words are being read, acolytes move throughout the chancel and the nave to light all of the candles in the church as symbolic action of the light of Christ illuminating the world. The service closes with the recessional hymn, "Rejoice! Rejoice! Emmanuel shall come to thee!"

The second Sunday after Epiphany is often observed as Missionary Day. Certainly, the missionary theme is one of the basic emphases of the Epiphany season. The illumination of the world, by the light of the Gospel of Christ, calls for missionary action. It means that someone will have to take the Gospel to the dark places. Therefore, January is often used as a missionary month. Ministers take advantage of this Epiphanytide theme by preaching their missionary sermons for the year.

Meanwhile, the first whole week in January is used in many communities as a Week of Prayer. It was felt that, following the first of the year, the Christian life of the community might be supported and helped if Christians everywhere sought God's help for the year through certain exercises of prayer and worship. It was also thought that if Christians had some notion of being supported in their prayer and worship by other people in other churches who were doing the same devotional exercises, that they would be strengthened. Therefore, many communities arrange union services during the weekday events of the Week of Prayer. Congregations will then move from one church to another to hear the pastors of the community preach upon the various aspects of prayer and the devotional life. Booklets of private prayers, written each year for the Week of Prayer, are distributed among the people and used by them. It must be said, however, that this custom of setting aside an entire week for this emphasis is not as popular today as formerly.

· february

During the month of February church attendance begins to increase and the whole parish program is accelerated as the calendar of worship moves toward Lent. Before Lent begins, however, several special days make their appearance. The Sunday nearest to Lincoln's birthday is often observed as Race Relations Sunday. Upon that occasion, ministers preach sermons which heavily underscore the need for tolerance between races. Here in the United States the status of the negro receives special attention. Many of the denominations take a special offering for negro work upon Race Relations Sunday. A report to the congregation is made concerning the various enterprises in which the denomination is engaged to lift the level of negro life in this country.

On the Sunday nearest Washington's birthday, worshiping congregations are taught to remember the essential brotherhood and family relationship of all mankind. Indeed, the day is called Brotherhood Sunday. It calls the attention of the people to the need for good relationships among the various social groups which people the city: Jews and Gentiles, old line Americans and new Americans. People of German, Swedish, Italian and English backgrounds are all part of the same community. When they understand one another and have some sense of their essential solidarity, the community itself is immeasurably strengthened. In many communities an interesting exchange of fellowship occurs on Brotherhood Sunday. Often Jewish rabbis will preach from the pulpits of Christian churches that day. The pastors of these same churches will speak in the Jewish synagogues the following Friday. Often Brotherhood Sunday is a prelude to Brotherhood Week. A joint dinner will be sponsored by the synagogue and churches of a community. There are many interesting possibilities that will give significance to this February Sunday as the idea takes firmer hold upon the churches.

· lent

At long last the ancient season of Lent begins. It is a period of quietness and meditation. At the same time, the parish program becomes richer and more varied than it appears at any time of the year. This paradox is the result of Protestant Christians' conviction that during Lent men and women ought to reduce their social program in order to give more time to private prayer and to those devotional services of the church which are designed to dilate one's understanding of religion and to relate one more truly to God.

For the Protestant, Lent becomes a renewal of his spent energy. Burdened by many responsibilities and sometimes confused by decisions which have to be made, the Lenten period offers a man a few weeks of quiet, meditative services in which insights are deepened and strength renewed. In the ancient words of Jesus, it says to the tired activist, "Come ye, into the desert and rest awhile."

This kind of a Lent rises out of man's recognition of his own need in the face of catastrophic forces. Today man feels that he lives in a world which is too gigantic to deal with successfully. Immense social forces seem to be catapulting him down into disaster. Protestant Christians know that what they need right now—and the whole world, too—is a new sense of personal strength and adequacy with which to meet the cyclonic social pressures of our day. They recognize the need for new confidence in the church as an instrument through which God may work with them for a better world. This sense of adequacy, for which they long, can come to them in particular, at least, during the Lenten program. To many a Christian and to many a church, Lent brings new understanding of the fact that God can use and does use each parish church and the whole church for his own useful purposes. No wonder that Lent brings a radiant sense of comradeship with the God of all hope and power, of whom the Bible declares, "The kingdoms of this world are become the kingdoms of our Lord, and of his Christ; and he shall reign for ever and ever."

The initial retreat which Jesus made at the beginning of his ministry forms the prototype for our Lenten pattern today. Following his baptism, Jesus at once sought the reality of God through long days devoted to prayer and meditation. Then Jesus rested his life upon the confidence, which came to him during the retreat, that God was truly alive in the world at work for the achievement of his divine purposes. With this confidence in God, the Gospel says that "Jesus returned in the power of the spirit into Galilee."

This kind of a Lenten program has been adapted to the ancient liturgical season of Lent celebrated by the historic churches. As everyone knows, the season originated in the early ages of Christianity. It formed part of the general Easter cycle which long had its vigils and days of fasting, the number of which varied with the time and place. Gregory I, at the close of the sixth century, fixed the beginning of Lent as Ash Wednesday, the sixth week before Easter and since then that has been the accepted beginning of the Lenten period. Lent lasted for forty days exclusive of Sundays. It was a period of special abstinence and attention to the exercises of religion. It culminated in Holy Week commemorating the passion and death of Jesus. Both its opening and closing days assume unusual solemnity. Traditionally, Ash Wednesday was a period of penitential prayer and fasting and Good Friday, which marked the real close of Lent, was such a solemn day that it was sometimes called Black Friday.

In the Protestant Church Ash Wednesday is celebrated in several different ways. The Episcopal Church uses the penitential office for Ash Wednesday, a special service which is found in the Book of Common Prayer. It is based upon the 51st Psalm, one of the old penitential psalms of the Hebrew people in which the worshiper cries out, "Have mercy upon me, O God, after thy great goodness, according to the multitude of thy mercies do away mine offences." It continues with the familiar Kyrie Eleison and the Lord's Prayer, the versicles and office collect. The penitential offices are often used in connection with Evening Prayer or Morning Prayer or in association with Holy Communion.

Sometimes Ash Wednesday is celebrated with Holy Communion. This is a growing practice in the Protestant Church. Often communions are spaced throughout the day to make them available for various groups of people in the parish. In other parishes, Evening Prayer is offered to the congregation. Sometimes this assumes the form of a special service for Ash Wednesday such as the one used in a Ripon parish church. The service is built around a three-fold pattern of worship. At first the weariness of the soul is recognized and an office collect read: "Almighty God, who in thy wisdom hast provided this Lenten retreat for weary souls, grant us the comfort of thy strengthening presence, we beseech thee; that our faith may be renewed, our despair be changed to hope and our sorrow be transformed into joy, through Jesus Christ our Lord, in whose memory and spirit we have met for holy worship. Amen." This is followed by a litany of despair in which the people cry out, "O Lord, hear our prayer and let our cry come unto thee."

After the choir sings the "Agnus Dei" the second movement of the service begins under the heading, "The Strength of God." If the soul is burdened by weariness and despair, a strong God is adequate to meet that need. This theme is announced in the reading of the 46th psalm, "God is our refuge and strength," continued in the gospel and the meditation of the minister, and given symbolic expression by the lighting of the candles in the sanctuary during the organ interlude.

The service concludes with the third movement called "The Renewal of Life." The minister reads such a psalm as the 121st in which the presence of God is set forth in those familiar words, "The Lord shall preserve thy going out and thy coming in from this time forth, and even for evermore." It is continued by the soloist who sings from "The Messiah," "He shall feed His flock, like a shepherd," and by responsive acts of confidence between minister and people. It concludes with the singing of the Doxology and the benediction. The congregation has had the experience in this service of sharing in quick dramatic action the essential pattern of recovery which the whole Lenten period makes possible.

On the Friday after Ash Wednesday, the Protestant women of the world have appropriated a day for their own use. It is called "The World Day of Prayer." It has come to be a very popular part of the Lenten celebration of Protestantism all over the world. On that day union services are held in each community which are largely attended by the women who have a strong sense of their solidarity with other Christian women in other communities and other nations. The same service of worship is used by the women of America that is used by Christian women in other parts of the world. A great circle of prayer girdles the world on that day. In the United States these services for the World Day of Prayer are supervised by the women's division of the National Council of Churches.

Meanwhile, the Lenten pattern assumes many forms in the Protestant Church. Every parish makes a special effort to deepen its religious life during Lent. To this end, additional touches appear during the Sunday morning service and many special meetings and services are arranged. Ministers are very much inclined to preach a series of sermons during Lent related to a common theme. Sermons on the Lord's Prayer, the Apostles' Creed and events in the life of Jesus are popular subjects. At one time or another the pastor is likely to build his Lenten sermons around these themes.

Midweek meetings of various kinds interest the parish. Some churches arrange special classes for study during Lent. Often these classes seek to awaken appreciation of some segment of Biblical literature, for missions, for church history or for the devotional life. Often Holy Communion is offered in the chapel as a special service each week during Lent. Sunday evenings or other occasions are set aside for cantatas, oratorios and other presentations of Lenten and Passion music.

One church offered a special Lenten service called "The Celebration of Christ the Lord." It was a recital in poetry, Scripture and music of the ministry of Jesus. Poetry and music set forth the events of the Nativity, the Galilean ministry, the Passion, the Resurrection and the presence of the living Christ in his church today. In these ways and many others special services bring to the minds of people the insights of Jesus into the nature of God and a new sense of confidence in Christian living. All of these services culminate in the dramatic movement of Holy Week.

Move here and there across the country to share in the amazing variety of the Lenten pattern. Take Old South Church in Boston as an example of Lent in the Congregational churches. During the 1952 season, the minister, Dr. Frederick Meek, preached a series of Sunday morning sermons under the vital, relevant topic: How Are We To Live In Days Like These? The general topic formed the title of the first sermon in the series. Other topics which he discussed in the series were, "Stop Resisting God," "Face the Attacks on the Faith," "Be Christian in a Sub-Christian World," "Fulfill the Disciplines of the Faith," and "Hold to the Best At Any Cost."

In addition to these Sunday morning sermons and services, the associate ministers provided a series of meditations on the psalms during a vesper service on Sunday. These meditations helped to deepen and enrich the devotional life of worshipers.

On Thursday evenings a Lenten supper was held for all the members of the parish. Following the supper, there was a School for Christian Living. Dr. Meek spoke each week on the general topic: In Training for Christian Living, and discussed such aspects of it as "Decision and Growth," "The Basis for Christian Social Action," "How Are We To Witness in Our Society," and others.

Students and other young adults united in a fellowship called "Old South Seminar." This group met Sunday evenings for supper and for discussion of the general topic: What a Christian Believes. Various religious leaders in Boston, and adjacent to it, came in to discuss this fundamental topic with Old South youth and young adults.

Meanwhile, certain special events enriched the Lenten program. These events included the Women's Guild Bible Study Course, instruction classes in church membership, several celebrations of Holy Communion and a service of Choral Vespers. Here was a great church, in one of the freest Protestant traditions, filling its life and program with significant Lenten emphases in terms of study, fellowship and worship.

Move from Boston to New York City to see what Christ Church, Methodist, is doing during Lent. This is the church of which the well known radio pastor, Dr. Ralph Sockman, is minister. During the season of 1952 Dr. Sockman preached a series of Sunday morning sermons on such topics as "The Peace of God," and "The Power of Patience." Many of these sermons were repeated later in the day at a vesper service. These Sunday services of worship always form the very heart of the Lenten program of any Protestant parish church and Christ Church is no exception to this general pattern. Still later in the day the church sponsors a program known as the "University of Life." This begins with a fellowship supper and continues with a series of study groups, including groups for young adults and high school students.

A particular midweek emphasis made by Christ Church centered on Wednesday evenings. It included a fellowship supper and was built around the general topic, "A Christian and His Daily Work." This took the form of a series of panel discussions by outstanding Christian laymen of New York who developed the topic, "What Difference the Christian Faith Makes in My Profession." In the field of business management, for example, the panel included Wesley F. Rennie, executive director of the Committee for Economic Development, Chester A. Barth, president of National Selected Products, Inc., Lee H. Hill, of Rogers, Slade and Hill, and Earl Newsom of the public relations firm by his name. Other panels were concerned with the field of public service, with the field of psychology, with women at work and the field of scientific research. This latter panel included Dr. Le Roy Kimball, vice-chancellor of New York University, Dr. John C. Kidd, pathologist of Cornell University, Dr. John R. Metcalf, with the research laboratories of Shell Oil Company and Dr. Harden F. Taylor, past president of the New York Academy of Science. Here was a vital expression of the interest of the church in the common life. Here was an excellent attempt to make religion relevant to what people are doing every day.

Look for a moment at another Lenten program in a Methodist church. Move a thousand miles west to a little town of 4000 people where Ripon College is located. Under the pastorate of Dr. Theodore Loeppert, the Ripon Methodist Church once organized its Lenten program around the general topic, "The Proposal of Jesus." It was one of the most carefully developed Lenten programs that one is likely to find. It was preceded by an invitation from the pastor, an invitation which established the theme of the program:

"Why should we reject the Proposal of Christ? Shall we let trifling inconveniences keep us from the Good News written in his life and words and sealed with his passion and blood? All creation turns toward us as the chosen children of men in the earnest expectation that we shall reveal His Presence in clarity and truth. How vain and stupid to let ordinary and transient things that wither and pass away quench the life and break down the structure of the soul which everyone knows is eternally disquieted until it rests in the Eternal!

"May this Eastertide help to estrange our sins from us. There are so many of them—self pride, complacency, indolence, jealousy, hatred, covetousness, narrow friendships, attitudes of superiority, social aversions, the willful stunting of personal growth, and many more. May we all be cleansed and brought to health and inner harmony through the Way, the Truth and the Life!"

The program concerning "The Proposal of Jesus" was divided into four parts. The first was introductory and offered an opportunity for evening prayer and for the celebration of Holy Communion.

The second part coincided with the second, third and fourth weeks of Lent. It was developed in terms of the theme, "The Life and Words of Jesus: the New Way." Sunday morning sermons set forth the initial proposals of Jesus to the people of his day. These proposals were further developed during Sunday evening services. On Wednesdays fellowship suppers were held and such specialized topics of Jesus' proposals were discussed as, "The Narrower Discipleship," "The Present and Eternal Resurrection," and "Have We Outgrown Missions?"

Jesus always sought a decision from people. This Lenten program was so announced that it, too, sought a definite decision which was done during the fifth week of Lent. Sunday morning and evening services moved in the direction of contrition, repentance and forgiveness. This emphasis was continued during the midweek services.

Holy Week and Easter brought this Lenten program to a close under the theme, "The New Life." On Sunday morning and on the evenings of Holy Week the pastor outlined the new life which the Christian found in Christ and the Church. This Holy Week program was enriched by the singing of Gounod's "Gallia" on Palm Sunday evening, Holy Communion on Thursday and the singing of Stainer's "Crucifixion" on the evening of Good Friday. The whole program achieved climactic splendor on Easter when the pastor preached on "The Great Joy of the Christian Religion," and the

Church School on Sunday evening presented one of Elliott Field's Easter plays.

Dr. Loeppert's suggestions for Christian behavior during Lent express some of the general emphases of Protestant churches throughout the country. Since he expresses them so well and with such devotional sensitiveness, it will be helpful to read them. They appeared as part of the Lenten program:

- "What to Do"
    A. Practice the presence of God through frequent prayer—just turn your heart to God, Who is there where you are. Pray for—
    —Your security in the face of life and death;
    —Your renewal and growth as a Christ-like person; that you may become his 'brother, mother, sister' through doing God's will (Mt. 12,50);
    —Those you love; those among whom you live; and those who look to you;
    —The renewal and expansion of the Christian community in the entire life of the world.
    B. As a token of your prayer put aside a sum of money each day, preferably denying yourself adornment, indulgence, personal property.

    C. Submit yourself to a careful self-examination, and through self-discipline, eliminate from your life useless and profitless and harmful practices and habits.

D. Set out now to find your place of service and expression in the Church and determine to do your part wtih your very best strength, devotion and intelligence.

E. Study the Book of the World with ceaseless application and look to the spiritual image and significance of Christ. Bring your questions out into the light and never let them rest. Accept no easy or mechanical answers—nor any that do not grip the heart of you. Give your very best to your problems and struggles, and seek proper guidance.

F. Release your soul through worship during the day's routine as well as in the frequently offered opportunities in the Sanctuary.

The Lutheran Church is, of course, one of the major branches of Protestantism. It has always preserved the best liturgical practices of antiquity. From the beginning, it has continued the celebration of Lent. Throughout the country, as well as in other parts of the world, each Lutheran parish church arranges the kind of a program in terms of worship that will benefit its particular congregation. Here is the Lenten program of the Evangelical Lutheran Church of the Holy Communion of Racine. It was arranged under the pastorate of Dr. G. W. Genszler. Sunday morning services brought a series of sermons by the pastor under the title, "The Glorious Cross." On Sunday evenings he presented what was called "heart to heart talks" on "What it Means to be a Christian." Wednesday evenings were devoted to a series of devotional studies on "The Shepherd Psalm." During Holy Week evening services were held which included confirmation of adults, two services of confession and absolution and the observance of the Lord's Supper on Maundy Thursday. This is typical of Lutheran programs, by and large, for they are inclined to make less of the social or fellowship aspects of Lent than the freer Protestant churches do. Furthermore, their Lenten topics are more inclined to remain within the framework of the Bible, rather than to lift up for consideration important aspects of the common life.

The other great branch of Protestantism that long has celebrated Lent in all of its richness is the Episcopal Church. One of the great Episcopal churches of the midwest is St. Luke's Church of Evanston, once led by the Reverend George Craig Stewart, its notable rector who later became bishop of Chicago. Perhaps the most interesting Lenten program ever to be devised in Chicagoland was under Dr. Stewart's direction. It was called "A Lenten Crusade." Since St. Luke's Church was a large Evanston church and several priests were on the staff, it was possible to fill almost every day with significant Lenten action. Notice how all of this action emerges out of the general theme of a Crusade. Like other Episcopal churches, Holy Communion was celebrated several times each Sunday and early in the morning every day of the week. Daily communion is a basic concept in a large segment of the Episcopal Church. A good Anglican who wants to keep Lent completely will make his daily communion and the parish church will provide the opportunity.

On Sunday mornings Dr. Stewart preached on "The Crusade Equipment," taking his sermon topics from the famous chapter of St. Paul. Such titles were taken from Paul as "The Girdle of Truth," "The Breastplate of Righteousness," "The Shield of Faith," "The Helmet of Salvation" and "The Sword of the Spirit." Sunday afternoons at Evensong, one of the other priests on the staff discussed the topic, "Youth and the Crusade."

Sunday afternoons, too, the rector had his course for the confirmation of men and women. On Monday evenings the rector offered another course under the title, "The Faith By Which We Live." On Tuesdays there was a children's service in the afternoon following school, with one of the assistant priests talking to the children about the great crusaders of the church, such as St. Martin, St. Hugh, St. Catherine and others. On Wednesdays there was a boys' class for confirmation in the afternoon and in the evening notable cantatas sung by the choir. For a choir to sing a whole cantata every week during Lent is really an outstanding achievement. This was made possible by the long time organist and choirmaster, Herbert Hyde, who was a man of exceptional ability. "The Story of the Cross" by Buck, "The Daughter of Jairus" by Stainer, "The Darkest Hour" by Moore, "The Crucifixion" by Stainer and other cantatas were sung. Thursday afternoons brought a service in the church in which the rector and one of his assistant priests presented a series of "Disputations on Great Questions." These two men would talk from the chancel on such topics as: "A Book or a Life," "Where is Jesus?" "Really or Spiritually?" and others. Friday brought a girls' class for confirmation and also a reading of the litany and devotional instruction in the matter of the Ideal Crusader. Holy Week presented the usual devotional and special services which are a part of the ancient liturgical office for the closing days of Lent. Here was something little short of tremendous for a Lenten program in a parish church. It greatly strengthened the church for its service to the community and to its own denomination.

Some of these features from that Lenten Crusade of yesterday are continued today by St. Luke's Church. Other features have been added as the Family Eucharist and parish breakfasts on the Sunday mornings during Lent. Mondays now bring a public service, presenting a familiar member of the adjacent seminary to discuss the message of the prophets. Services of benediction have been added to part of the evening program.

These examples, from a few churches throughout the

· 91

country, emphasize the fact again that Protestant Christianity celebrates Lent in many different ways. They underline the fact that the church is alert to this annual cycle as a means of strengthening its understanding and making sure that the bonds between man and God will hold.

• holy week

In many ways Holy Week is the most dramatic movement of the church year. It is bound to be dramatic in its nature for it recapitulates the events in the last week of Jesus' life. These events are set forth in such details in the gospels and are of such crucial importance to the ministry of Jesus and the fellowship of the church that they are remembered every year with affection. The early apostolic group were so deeply impressed by this last week that they remembered it in all of its rich detail. Their memory became part of the cycle in the oral tradition. Later on it was recorded by Mark to become part of the gospel record itself.

The traditional interpretation of Holy Week marks its beginning with the entrance of Jesus into the city of Jerusalem. He rode upon a donkey, symbolic of peace and humility. The many disciples who accompanied him and who greeted his entrance into the city cried out with spontaneous alleluias, singing, "Hosanna; blessed is he that cometh in the name of the Lord. Hosanna in the highest!" Following the inspection of the temple area, Jesus returned to the home of his friends in Bethany, a suburb of Jerusalem. There he conferred with them and planned his strategy for the remainder of the week. He had decided to take his message from Galilee to the center of Jewish life and culture to the capital itself. He had picked the season of the Passover as the best moment in which to challenge the authority of the ecclesiastical leaders of Israel. He wanted to do this in the presence of large numbers of Jews who came to Jerusalem every year for the Passover celebration. The authorities took advantage of the pilgrimage of the faithful by charging them at many points, particularly at the vital point of their pilgrimage when they exchanged the coin of their native realm for Jewish money which alone was acceptable for the purchase of a sacrificial animal. Jesus was greatly concerned on his visit to the temple area on the first day of the week to find the entire system of money exchange and the sale of animals set up in the temple precincts itself. Part of his strategy would include the dramatic challenge of the right of the authorities thus to use the temple area.

On Monday, he and his apostles and many of the disciples went directly to the temple where they overturned the tables of the petty bankers who were exchanging money. He drove out those who bought and sold the sacrificial animals. Then he gathered the people around him and declared, "My house shall be called a house of prayer; but ye have made it a den of thieves." The gospel records that then the blind and the lame came to him in the temple and he healed them and the children cried out, "Hosanna, to the son of David."

On Tuesday he returned to Jerusalem to be challenged in turn by the temple authorities. They sought to involve him in public controversy by asking by what authority he acted and spoke. They tried to involve him in unfriendly remarks toward the imperial power by asking whether they should pay tribute to Caesar or not. He answered their questions and turned upon them in a series of denunciations that must have stung like a lash and cut like a whetted knife.

Wednesday has been interpreted traditionally as a day of silence which Jesus spent in Bethany with his friends. There he sought strength and guidance for the future. On that evening occurred a beautiful happening when the woman anointed him with fragrant ointment and he interpreted it as a faithful and charming gesture. Said he, "She hath done what she could. She has come aforehand to anoint my body to the burying."

On Thursday evening Jesus celebrated the Passover feast in the Upper Room of a Jewish friend. He used the occasion to fix upon their minds a pattern of a memorial service which later they were to perform in memory of him. When he broke the bread and the meat of the feast, he said, "This is my body." When he blessed and passed the cup of wine, he said, "This is my blood of the new covenant which is shed for you and for many for the remission of sins." He used the occasion for another symbolic gesture. He girded himself with a towel and washed the feet of his disciples to illustrate the meaning of the ministry of service. After supper he discoursed at length concerning the Kingdom of God. Then he left with his apostles for the city park known as Gethsemane. Under the luminous stars, with the warm wind blowing, he made his final decision to live or not to live, to flee back to Galilee or to follow his strategy to the very end, which now appeared to be the cross. Even while he finished his search for guidance, the police of the ecclesiastical authorities broke into the garden, arrested him and took him back to the Sandedrin for trial. On Friday he was brought before the Roman governor, condemned to death and crucified on a skull-shaped mound outside of the city. His body was released by Pilate to a friend and placed in the tomb of Joseph of Arimathea for later burial.

Very early these events of Holy Week were dramatized into liturgical services of the church. Roman Catholic Christianity has a complete set of offices for these various days. Preceding the mass on Palm Sunday is a service called "The Blessing of the Psalms" which includes a number of superb prayers relating to the imagery of the psalms, the procession with choir and clergy into the church singing the magnificant hymn, "Gloria, laus, et honor tibi sit, Rex Christe, Redemptor." Then the service moves into the opening phase of the mass. The daily offices and mass continue as usual for Monday and Tuesday when the events of Holy Week are recapitulated. On Wednesday evening Tenebrae is read, the night office for the last three days of Holy Week, consisting of a series of psalms, antiphons and the lessons and using the dramatic imagery of the extinguishing of the candles. On Thursday a simple mass in memory of the institution of the Lord's Supper is celebrated and the holy oils for healing are blessed. On Friday the popular Tre Ore services are held, a three hour vigil from noon until three o'clock in the afternoon in commemoration of the three hours Jesus hung upon the cross.

In the Lutheran and Episcopal churches many of these services were modified and retained. Palms are distributed on Palm Sunday morning in the Episcopal churches, services and meetings are held each day, though on Friday the Episcopal Church, like the Roman Catholic Church, celebrates only a dry mass. There is no consecration or consumption of the bread and wine, except in Anglo-Catholic churches where the priest communicates from the sacred elements which have been reserved in the tabernacle from yesterday's mass. In the Episcopal Church, too, the oils are often blessed on Thursday and Tenebrae is observed on Wednesday and Thursday evenings. The old and dramatic ritual of the Lutheran and Anglican churches set forth in rich detail the events of Holy Week.

In recent years many of these services have been used by the other branches of Protestant Christianity. The freer churches have come to feel that by these services of commemoration and dramatic action, a reasonable and reverent way can be found to enter into the passion story of Jesus. At first there were hesitant gestures in this direction. By the turn of the century Dr. John Hunter of Scotland, in his book of devotional services at Trinity Church, Glasgow, included thematic prayers for the various days of Holy Week. Dr. William

Orchard, at the Congregational Chapel of London, known as the King's Weighhouse Church, included in his book of worship the Tenebrae service for Maundy Thursday and a special litany for Good Friday, which included the adoration of the cross.

A typical parish program for Holy Week includes a festival service on Palm Sunday with the choir singing the festival hymn of Theodulph of Orleans, "All glory, laud and honor, to Thee, Redeemer, King." Evening services are held on Monday, Tuesday and Wednesday in which the minister's meditations recapitulate the events in the life of Jesus on those particular days and the significance of those events for the world. Sometimes these services assume the dramatic form of the old ritual of Tenebrae. On Thursday evening the Lord's Supper is celebrated in memory of that distant event when Jesus instituted this ceremonial meal. This observance of the Lord's Supper is often combined with Tenebrae. As the service moves to a close, the lights of the church and the candles of the altar are extinguished to symbolize the darkness which came upon the world when the Light of life was put out. On Friday evening often one of the Passion oratorios is sung, such as Stainer's Crucifixion, or Buck's "Story of the Cross."

In addition to these evening services, often Protestant churches will unite for a series of noon day services. These are held either in a theater or a downtown church. Sometimes a visiting pastor of prominence will be engaged to give the noon day meditations. Protestant businessmen and women come to this place of worship

each noon and for a few minutes make an act of re-
collection concerning the last week of Jesus' life. This
noonday service concludes with the great three hour
service on Friday in which the ministers of the community participate. Often this service is built around
the seven last words of Jesus with each minister giving
a meditation upon one of these words. Preceding and
following the meditations are appropriate hymns and
prayers. At other times, the three hour period is divided
into units of one hour each, each one of which is used
to present a complete service of worship in the development of some three-fold theme, such as Jesus Christ:
Prophet, Priest and King.

Some of these services bring the passion events to unusual dramatic fulfillment. This is particularly true
concerning the services on Thursday and Friday. In the
new Book of Worship, used by the Congregational-
Christian Churches in the United States, there is a
vigil outlined for Maundy Thursday which uses the
old ceremonial of the office of Tenebrae combined with
the Holy Communion. Worshipers enter the dimly
lighted church and find that the communion table is
prepared for Holy Communion and that an additional
table has been added to it to form the letter T. In the
center of the altar is placed a single conspicuous candle
which is lighted. Along the two sides of the lower
table, which forms the base of the letter T, are eight
chairs for the deacons. At each place is a small lighted
candle and a card containing certain scriptural passages
which are to be read. After the communion service is
over, the deacons take their assigned places at the tables

and begin to read from their scripture cards the story of the events of that ancient historic night. As each deacon finishes his reading he extinguishes his candle. Synchronizing with the extinguishing of the candles is the slow dimming of the lights of the church. As the last lesson is read the church is in darkness except for the single candle at the center of the altar. Finally, that is put out by the minister. After a few moments of darkness, the minister relights the center candle. Very dimly the lights of the church are turned on as symbolic of the fact that Easter is soon to dawn.

This same Book of Worship, and also the Book of Worship used by the Methodist Church, contains an extended order of worship for the Good Friday service. In the Methodist Book of Worship the three hour service for Good Friday is built around the seven last words of Jesus. It includes calls of worship and invocation, collect for the day, appropriate anthems, confession of sin and assurance of forgiveness, together with the seven words from the cross, each one preceded and followed by a hymn and prayers.

One of the most interesting of these Good Friday services has been devised by William Norman Guthrie, who for many years was rector of St. Mark's Church in the Bouwerie. He called his service "Seven Oracles from the Cross." It was a wonderfully original conception of the Good Friday service, a prototype of better things to come in the Protestant Church as creative artists, unhampered by tradition, allow their minds to work upon this Good Friday material and bring it to superb liturgical expression.

This service begins with an introduction, containing certain collects for the day, a litany of adoration between minister and the people, using the response,

·   "Jesus, my Lord, I thee adore,
    Make me to love thee more and more."

Following this introduction, the meditations on the seven words begin. The first meditation is broken in the middle by a poem of aspiration. It concludes with another poem, a group of collects and a liturgical conceit with chimes, which enable choir and organist gently, hesitantly and suggestively to maintain the prevailing mood and to act as transitions between the movements of the service. Other poems from William Blake and St. Theresa enrich these moments of transition and interlude. The second word is announced and developed. Again the collects and the chimes and a ballad of Ezra Pound bring it to a close. Thus the service moves through the seven words of Jesus from the cross. Concluding at length with the adoration and the old litany of victory by William Blake, using the refrain, "O Lord, give us the victory," and a hymn on the glory of the cross brings this dithyrambic service to a close.

When the final bells have tolled on Good Friday, Lent is over and the winter cycle is done. Saturday of Holy Week is a strange interlude in the calendar of worship of the church. It was during Saturday that Jesus' body lay in the tomb. It was the only day of his ministry that he was not alive and present with his friends and his church. What can the church do on

Holy Saturday but to wait . . . and wait, for the inevitable resurrection which it is confident will occur?
In anticipation of that resurrection, sometimes there is
observed a modern adaptation of an ancient liturgical
service which comes from the early centuries, known
as "Lucernarium," the ancient service of lights at which
the new fire is blessed. That, however, is a prelude to
Easter and belongs with the next chapter.

Almighty God,

who hast taught us that in quietness and confidence shall be our strength, we thank Thee for these Lenten days. We are glad for these quiet moments of worship when we seek to enter the world of the spirit, there to behold Thy heavenly glory and to consider Thy will for us. We rejoice in the confidence which comes to us while we wait and wonder and lift up our hearts to Thee. All the week this confidence undergirds us in the decisions which must be made, the work by which we earn our bread and the problems which appear. All the week we are glad that in the quietness and confidence of worship, Thy strength and Thy Presence dost come to prepare us for all that must be done.

Grant us unusually clear minds, we beseech Thee, for the facing and understanding of those great issues of our day which mean all the difference between life and death, between fruitful peace and awful war. Free our minds from all prejudice and hatred, from fear and selfishness as we think about our relations with the rest of the world. Enable us to put aside the folly of greed, the sin of party prejudice and the false security of our own good fortune as a nation. Open our eyes to all the consequences of those actions which now we plan to take. Speak to us in a clear voice about those ways which truly will make for peace. And let the will of the people and Thine own Divine Will be felt in the mind and heart of our president and all his advisors that the terror of war may be averted.

Meanwhile, we are grateful beyond all words to express, for Thy continued ministry to our needs. Heal the sick, we beseech Thee. Comfort the sorrowful. Encourage the timid. Shame the selfish. Confound the trouble-maker. Illuminate our desolate moments with Thy light and love, and grant us the comfort of Thy Presence always; through Jesus Christ our Lord.

Amen.

^ the spring cycle

"O Wind,
If winter comes, can spring be far behind?"
The hope and the longing expressed in those
fine old words of Shelley come to marvelous fulfillment in the spring cycle of the Protestant Church. The
first fluted notes of Easter's early dawn are the wel-
come sounds of the spring forest and the river glen, the
lake shore and the dunes along the sea. These sounds
reflect the vitality and the urgency of the fundamental
force of life itself. Life speaks through the animation of
spring and the triumph of Easter to give man hope
again.

Easter is the Festival of the Resurrection and is one
of the oldest festivals in Christendom. Originally, the
Easter festival was called "Pascha" because it was associated with the Paschal Feast, the passover of the Jews.
The word Easter is the northern designation, made
much later from the old English "Eostre," the goddess
of spring. This great festival soon became the pivotal
moment in the whole calendar of worship. If there
had been no resurrection, there would not have been

the Christian movement as the early church knew very well. From the first age of Christianity to the present, therefore, the Festival of the Resurrection has been celebrated with jubilant hearts and all the resources of the liturgical arts.

In the olden days the Easter festival was anticipated by the vesper service and vigil of Saturday. Some of these services were built upon the ancient service of lights known as the "Lucernarium," at which the new fire of the night was blessed. This service is still used by the Roman Catholic Church today in its office for Holy Week. The service begins with interesting ceremonial in the narthex of the church where the new fire is lighted and a triple taper, representing the Holy Trinity, is elevated to lead the great processional from narthex to sanctuary. Beautiful prayers and litanies are said which symbolize the return of light to the world in the resurrection of Jesus Christ.

These First Vespers of Easter have been adapted to Protestant usage and now form the prelude to the Easter festival in certain Protestant parishes. A good many Episcopal churches, for example, schedule the First Vespers of Easter and the lighting of the paschal candle as an afternoon service for Holy Saturday. In the academic chapels of the Episcopal Church, such as the chapel of the theological seminary at Nashota House, this is a very beautiful service. The new fire is struck with a piece of flint in the narthex of the chapel. To the accompaniment of Gregorian plain chant, sung by the students in beautiful antiphonal singing, the procession moves into the chancel where the interesting ceremonial takes place. Pieces of incense are inserted into the Paschal candle in the form of a cross. The whole sanctuary is dusted with incense and the candles of the chapel are lighted as the service comes to its close.

There is another adaptation of this ancient service available for the freer forms of Protestantism. It begins with the reading of the litany at the rear of the nave. The prophecies of the Messiah are read by the minister and the triple cluster of candles is lighted and held aloft. Minister, deacons and choir then move to the foot of the chancel where the deacon reads the passion lessons from prophecy, and hymn of the passion is sung. Then the procession moves into the chancel itself and the choristers take their places in the choir stalls and the cluster of lights is placed in the candle holder on the altar. Then the collect for Easter is read:

"Almighty God, from whose radiant Being streams of life forever flow, and whose paternal compassion has granted to the world the resurrection of Jesus, grant that the light of his presence may now go forth to all mankind; that they may see the truth more clearly, live more perfectly and finally receive the blessing of eternal life with thee; through Jesus Christ our Lord. Amen."

During this reading the minister goes to the altar and hands the light to acolytes who proceed to light all the candles in the church while the minister and deacon adorn the altar with its festival coverings. Following this, the lyric litany responsively is read, beginning with the words:

.   "O glory of the evening lights
Which shine at close of Holy Week.
O splendor of the western skies
Which speak to us of tomorrow's morn.
O beauty of the evening stars
Which burn in heaven on Easter Eve.

and ends with the couplet:

.   "O beauty of this Easter morn
In which our hope again is born."

The service closes with the Easter hymn and Holy Communion or baptism if the parish desires.

Other preludial Easter services have been immensely popular. Some of them have been carried to all parts of the country by radio, such as the community service held in Colorado's Garden of the Gods. There, to the accompaniment of the singing of birds and the crimson streamers of the rising sun, the neighboring community greets Easter in this majestic setting. Various pastors and choristers read and sing the festival liturgy which gives brightness, not only to the congregation assembled, but to eager listeners throughout the United States.

Similar services have been held in Soldiers' Field, Chicago, and in the parks and on the mountainsides and lakeshores of innumerable settings and places where youth, especially, have gathered to greet the Easter dawn with trumpets and hallelujahs.

In those parts of the country where the weather is not dependable, these services are often held in the church itself. Typical of these services is the Easter dawn baptismal service at the Baptist Temple of Philadelphia where Dr. Daniel Poling is the well-known pastor. The service of baptism is an important rite within the Baptist churches of America. Easter Day is often set aside for this rite of admittance into the Baptist fellowship. In those places where great crowds of people come to the regular morning service, which would be the case at the Baptist Temple, the early dawn service is used for this more intimate family experience of baptism.

Often youth unites with adulthood in sponsoring this sunrise service. The youth choirs sing a portion of the liturgy and the pastor will preach a brief sermon especially keyed to the interest and needs of youth. Sometimes Holy Communion is celebrated in this breathless moment of dawn. In many cases the worshipers participating in this early service will then gather in the parish house for an Easter breakfast.

It is during the chief Sunday morning service, however, that the full glory of Easter is celebrated in the Protestant churches. Every liturgical resource is brought to this superb moment in the calendar of worship. The church knows that if there had been no resurrection there would have been no Christian movement. It was the confidence of the apostles and disciples that Jesus had survived the shock of death and that his living Presence entered their fellowship again with such assurance to them that they went about announcing the glad news: He is arisen! This is the resurrection faith which is given magnificent expression on Easter morning.

Common to all Protestant churches are certain portions of the Easter liturgy. Up and down the country Protestant congregations are likely to sing for their Easter processional the stirring hymn of Charles Wesley:

> "Christ the Lord is risen today, Alleluia!
> Sons of men and angels say, Alleluia!
> Raise your joys and triumphs high,
>   Alleluia!
> Sing, ye heavens, and earth reply,
>   Alleluia!

Another favorite hymn at the Sunday morning service is that very ancient one from the eighth century by John of Damascus:

> "Come, ye faithful, raise the strain
> Of triumphant gladness;
> God hath brought His people forth
> Into joy from sadness.
> Now rejoice, Jerusalem,
> And with true affection
> Welcome in unwearied strains
> Jesus' resurrection."

Other portions of the liturgy come to this Easter service through the lessons, prayers and Easter sermon. The four gospels provide a variety of Easter narrative from which the minister may choose his lesson for the day. Because these gospel stories have been read so many times they are all familiar to our Protestant congregations. When the confident old words are read which announce the resurrection of Jesus and his repeated appearances to various groups of disciples, the old reassurance expressed by Jesus' friends takes possession of the modern congregation. Though every Protestant minister is likely to formulate his own Easter prayer, the same concepts tend to appear in all the prayers of Christendom on that festival morning: praise and adoration to the risen and living Christ, thanksgiving to God for the gift of immortality and certain petitions and intercessions for man's possession of triumphant faith. The collect for Easter Day in Morning Prayer sets the general theme for the free prayers which ministers offer during the Easter liturgy: "O God, who for our redemption didst give thine only begotten Son to the death of the cross, and by the glorious resurrection hast delivered us from the power of the enemy; grant us so to die, delivered from sin, that we may evermore live with him in the joy of his resurrection; through the same Christ our Lord. Amen."

Easter sermons discuss such festival resurrection themes as, "The Christian Hope," "The Christian Faith in Immortality," "The Triumph of Goodness Over Evil" and "The Power Which Belongs to the Forces of God." Among the topics which Dr. Ernest Fremont Tittle discussed during his ministry at the First Methodist Church of Evanston were, "The Christian Hope of Immortality," "Thine is the Kingdom, the Power and the Glory," "The Triumph of God," "Resurrection" and repeatedly, the simple topic, "Immortality."

There is also a growing practice in the use of Handel's "Hallelujah Chorus" at the close of the service. Very thrilling it is when the sermon is over for the choirs and congregation to rise for that wonderful chorus which has the power to lift the human spirit in those clarion words, "Hallelujah! The kingdom of this world has become the kingdom of our Lord and of his Christ and he shall reign for ever and ever. King of kings, and Lord of lords! Hallelujah!"

Sometimes the Easter liturgy for Sunday morning receives very special development. In Los Angeles the Wilshire Methodist Church has a superb liturgical service which opens with trumpets and organ and an Easter introit sung by the cathedral choir. Then the service proper begins with the festival procession of the five choirs of the church: the cathedral, chancel, chapel and cantus choirs and the Wesleyan singers.

Following their festival hymn, "Christ the Lord is Risen Today," the second movement of worship begins, called "The Period of Decision." It opens with "The Hour of Decision in Music," an anthem sung by the five combined choirs:

> "Behold, thy King draws near the city gates!
> Go forth, Jerusalem, with shout and song."

This is continued in the responsive reading and "The Hour of Accomplishment in Music," sung by a base soloist. The minister then offers his own prayer which is followed by a dramatic reading setting forth "The Hour of Victory in Prose," an episode from Lloyd

Douglas' "The Robe." The minister then gives this "Hour of Victory" added resonance and tonality in his festival sermon of the day. This is then brought to full choral expression by the cathedral choir in a "Hymn Exultant."

The service then moves into its third phase, "The Period of Dedication." This is given outward and visible expression through the Easter offering which is presented at the chancel with prayers of thanksgiving, choral response and the Doxology. Then the service is brought to final and climactic expression in the "Hallelujah Chorus."

Another great Easter service is that held in the Fourth Presbyterian Church of Chicago, one of the great metropolitan churches on Michigan Boulevard with a beautiful French Gothic building. At the chief service in the nave the chancel choir sings the resurrection anthem following congregational acts of reading and singing. The minister then reads the lessons for the day and offers his pastoral prayer. Carols are then sung by the choir, the congregational offering is received and presented at the chancel while the offertory anthem is sung. The congregation then sings the preparatory hymn for the sermon, "Come, ye faithful, raise the strain," and the minister preaches on "The Fact of the Resurrection." After his post-service prayer and choral response, the service closes with the Easter hymn and benediction.

The Fourth Presbyterian Church is typical of many churches in the variety of worship presented on Easter Day. Early in the morning there is a liturgical service at which the minister preaches the same sermon that he uses at the chief service of the day. Simultaneously with the chief morning service, there is a chapel service in the Westminster Chapel led by one of the associate pastors and by other choirs of the church. This additional service, simultaneous with the chief service, is an accommodation to the large numbers of worshipers who cannot get into the nave. In the afternoon there is a Vesper Service and organ recital with emphasis upon Easter music. The day closes in the evening with a full liturgical service and sermon by another of the associate pastors. Here is a full, rich observance of Easter Day by one of the great Protestant churches of the country.

This variety in the celebration of Easter assumes many forms. The day will often open with a sunrise service. The afternoon will often bring vesper services with emphasis either upon music or meditation. Sometimes there will be a special vesper service of Holy Baptism. The evening may bring an Easter drama either in the parish house or in the chancel of the church itself, after the manner of the old morality players. In other parishes the choir may sing an Easter cantata or present some other form of choral festival worship. Take another example of the rather complete way in which a parish church may observe Easter, that of Epworth-Euclid Church of Cleveland. This congregation meets in a notable Gothic building, designed by Goodhue, and is served, as pastor, by one of the finest students of worship in the country, Dr. Oscar Thomas Olson. Easter begins with an early sunrise

service which uses a fine call to worship, collect and
litany of praise. The Vesper Choir sings the Easter
music and one of the associate pastors preaches the
sermon. This sunrise service then moves into the second service of Easter Day, the celebration of Holy Communion which incorporates a special Easter litany of
remembrance, beginning with the words:

> "O God who art the Father of all, grant
> Thy blessing upon us who are gathered
> here, and upon the multitudes of every
> name who are joined with us in one house-
> hold of faith through the world."

Following the consecration and the communion of the
people, the service closes with the Coronation Hymn.

The chief service of the morning is presented at two
different times to accommodate the great congregation
who want to worship on Easter. It is a full liturgical
service with ample musical expression of the Easter
theme by the choirs and soloists of the church, together
with the minister's festival sermon. In the afternoon
there is a Vesper Service, sung by the Junior and Tower
choirs of the church. As part of this service Holy Baptism is celebrated. Many families take advantage of the
Easter Day service to bring their children to the font
made sacred by the living Christ. The day closes with
the evening service which uses the beautiful Emmaus
Litany, an office for Eastertide. This litany begins with
the words: "By the love with which thou didst draw
near to thy disciples as they went to Emmaus and
talked together of thy Passion; draw near and join

thyself to us and give us a knowledge of thyself." To this versicle, the people respond, "Hear us, Blessed Jesus." The final response of the people is, "May the peace which thou gavest to thine Apostles, sending them forth in thy Father's Name as thou thyself was sent, be also upon us, and remain with us always. Amen." This evening service then moves into the presentation of the Easter drama by the Epworth-Euclid players.

Reluctantly, the Protestant Church watches Easter Day come to a close. Many a worshiper goes back to his parish church late in the afternoon or sits quietly before his household shrine at night to remember again the glory of the day: Resurgent life followed the crimson streamers of the dawn to awaken mankind with new hope . . . Brilliant trumpets and joyous alleluias announced the confident news, "He is Arisen" . . . Lovely carols and beautiful stories from the long ago touched the heart and brought a new sense of security and relaxation . . . The church crowded with eager worshipers spoke of the continued power of the living Christ . . . And now the solitary worshiper thanks God for it all in the fine words of the Nunc Dimittis, "Lord, now lettest thou thy servant depart in peace, according to thy word. For mine eyes have seen thy salvation. Which thou hast prepared before the face of all people; To be a light to lighten the Gentiles and to be the glory of thy people, Israel."

Then this solitary worshiper is very much inclined to pray in his own personal way, "Grant that thy grace may also heal this tired, suffering world in which we live, that all over this world men and women may unite to bring mankind to a new birth of hope and security and goodwill. So may there be upon this earth once more, a renewal of the old and loving way, the resurrection of life itself, the return of hope in that better world of which the poets have sung and the prophets have spoken and for which the Lord Christ both lived and died; through Jesus Christ our Lord. Amen."

· the festival of the christian home

Back in 1907 Miss Anna Jarvis of Philadelphia suggested the observance of Mother's Day to a parish church in a Virginia town in which her deceased mother had long been a moving spirit. The kind of a simple service which was arranged caught the imagination of people who wanted to honor their mothers and the whole idea of motherhood itself. Within a few years the Congress of the United States passed a resolution commending the observance of Mother's Day. In 1914 Congress authorized the president to set aside the second Sunday in May as Mother's Day.

For many years this day was observed by the Protestant churches of our land. Many a sermon was preached on this topic to the accompaniment of copious weeping on the part of receptive congregations. Indeed, the situation was often so heart moving that many a Protestant stayed home on Mother's Day because he could not hold up under the emotional strain. Other people made it a point to go to church on that day because they liked the sentiment and the drama that went with its observance. Pastors read lessons from the Bibles their mothers had given them, solos were sung which tore the cords of one's heart and many a Ladies' Aid distributed carnations to every mother who passed through the portals of the church that day.

At long last, the day was rescued for sane observance by the Commission on Worship of the Federal Council of Churches of Christ. This group suggested a change from Mother's Day to the Festival of the Christian Home. Immediately the base of the day was immeasurably broadened by this more comprehensive theme. Because the entire family was now included, the accent was no longer on motherhood itself and the temptation toward sentimentality was thus averted.

An increasing number of Protestant churches are now using the second Sunday in May in which to celebrate the Festival of the Christian Home. Sermons are preached which attempt to help the various members of American households to develop those attitudes and patterns of action that will inspire them to live normal and responsible lives. This is an important emphasis from any point of view for Judaism and Christianity, in Protestant and Catholic forms, are convinced that the basis of an effective American life is the solidarity of the American home. Organized religion is convinced of the fact that the maintenance of religion and the development of its ideals concerning character are dependent upon the religious expression of the household. For this reason, the insertion of the Festival of the

Christian Home in its calendar of worship is an important contribution of Protestantism.

• rural life sunday

For many years Protestant churches in rural areas and country towns have sought to call attention to the religious significance of the spring planting and the countryside. They have been aware of the fact that the entire economy of the nation is dependent upon the conservation and careful use of its land resources. The Church has united with the scientific conservation forces of university and government in studying the problem of land and its use. You cannot waste the land, allow the rich top soil to be carried away by the forces of erosion or mine it of essential crop minerals without replenishing them through scientific fertilization and have any sense of partnership with God. The Church believes that God is the Providence who has given us the good earth, appointed us as stewards in its care and use and holds us accountable for its conservation. All of this our rural pastors seek to clarify in their preaching. They have found that the observance of a Rural Life Sunday is a good time in which to do this.

When the Commission on Worship of the Federal Council of Churches published its initial outline of the Christian year, it designated the third Sunday in May as Rural Life Sunday. Since then much of this discussion and many observances of the importance of the land and the task of the farmer are given expression on this particular day.

Sometimes this expression takes the form of a full liturgical service which celebrates the Spring Planting. Typical of these celebrations is the liturgy of the Spring Planting used by the little community church of Greenbush, set among the Kettle Moraine Hills of Wisconsin. In a beautiful little Colonial church the worshipers gather together for the service which exalts the religious significance of all the work on the farms in the hills that surround the church. The service begins with an introit and hymn. It moves into the confession of sin and some lections of spring which are read alternately by the pastor and the deacon. These lections of spring are a group of poems which gather up the work of the farm and the glory of partnership with God in using his providence to the best advantage.

This concept is further developed by the Scripture lesson and the sermon. Following the sermon there is a confession of faith which affirms this partnership between God and man in regard to the brotherhood of the farm. The service comes to a close with the offering and a litany of dedication. This litany sets forth the task of the farmer in words like these:

> To God, our eternal Father, the creator
> and giver of all good things
>   We consecrate our gifts.
> To the teaching of Jesus and the building
> of his kingdom
>   We consecrate our gifts.
> To a life of increasing service to men
>   We dedicate ourselves.

the spring cycle

To the production of the basic needs of
  the world
    We dedicate ourselves.
To the farm, with its many possibilities
    We dedicate ourselves.
To the improvement of the country
    We dedicate ourselves.
In the planting of spring and the work
  that we do
    We earnestly beseech thy help.
The Lord's Prayer

·   memorial day

Because of its interest in the religious significance of the civil calendar, particularly in those days
set aside for national observance, the Protestant Church
shares in this recognition of Memorial Day. Often community services are held in the churches on the Sunday
nearest to the civil holiday. Patriotic groups will meet
in a body in a given parish church. Stirring national
hymns and anthems are sung, sermons are pitched to
one of several keys. Sometimes they seek to honor all
the blessed dead who have paid "the last full measure
of devotion" in the service of their country. The sermon will often close with an exhortation to be true to
the men who made this sacrifice, either in the Civil
War or in the World Wars of our own day.

·   "Take up our quarrel with the foe;
          To you from failing hands we throw
          The torch; be yours to hold it high."

Such a sermon, for example, is that by Ernest Fremont Tittle called "The Unfinished Task," which begins with the words, "It is no new idea that the valiant dead must look to us for the realization of ends for which they laid the world away." It points out the need for working in our day on the problem of peace. It affirms the fact that war can be abolished if we are prepared to give attention to the needs of others as well as our own needs. In closing, Dr. Tittle says, "Whatever others may do or fail to do, we must do what we can to establish a just and lasting peace; we must keep faith with the dead."

Other sermons preached on Memorial Day may reflect the interest of the church in current national action and in the problems which the nation faces. The religious significance of these problems is lifted up for consideration and the resources of religion are brought to their solution. This observance of Memorial Day is a vital part of Protestantism's calendar of worship and will remain in the liturgical year for a long time.

· children and youth

One of the days beloved by many a Protestant Church is observed on the second Sunday in June and is called Children's Day. At that time recognition is given to the place of children in the church and to the importance of the religious education program of the parish. In the old days this observance was always made during the morning service of the day with the adult congregation present. Often the Sunday School presented a miscellaneous program of songs and recitations. The more ambitious Church Schools might present a playlet or series of tableaux or in other ways give more extended expression to the interest of children.

Of course, Children's Day is really a very old observance for children's sermons were preached and children's activities given recognition in the service for a great many years. In 1856, however, Dr. Charles H. Leonard, pastor of the First Universalist Church of Chelsea, Massachusetts, designated a Sunday in which parents would bring their children for dedication and in which parents then would dedicate their time and thought to the careful religious nurture of these children. Dr. Leonard picked the second Sunday in June for this service. By 1868 the Methodist Episcopal Church took hold of this idea in its General Conference which recommended that Children's Day be observed annually on the second Sunday in June. By 1867 the Universalist convention at Baltimore passed a resolution, "Resolved, that we commend the parents of those churches in our order that set apart one Sunday in each year as Children's Day, when parents bring to the altar their most precious treasures and give them to the Lord by proper and sacred rites." By 1883 both the Presbyterian General Assembly and the National Council of Congregational Churches had made similar recommendations. No wonder that Children's Day became a popular feature of Protestant worship.

Children's Day is more likely to be observed in the various departments of the Church School itself. If recognition is given to it during the morning service of

the parish, it is more likely to be done by the pastor
with perhaps one or two of the youth of the church
assisting him in the reading of the lessons and responsive readings. He may then preach a sermon on Christian nurture or the rights of childhood under such a
topic as "Children are People, Too."

In June many churches observe a Baccalaureate Sunday to coincide with the graduation of their young
people from the high school of the community. Sometimes the baccalaureate service is actually sponsored by
the high school on the basis of a rotating system among
the churches of the community. In other towns the
high school will sponsor a baccalaureate service on
Sunday afternoon in its own auditorium. Various ministers of the community will take charge of the service
and one of them will preach. More and more, however,
parish churches are honoring their own graduates with
a baccalaureate service during Morning Worship. The
graduates and their parents meet before the service begins in one of the rooms of the church to form a procession with the choir. They march into the church
singing the processional hymn with the choristers and
take places in the front of the nave set apart for them.
Their names are listed on the calendar for the day and
the minister will express the interest of the congregation in their progress and will offer petitions to God
during his prayer for God's encouragement and direction in their lives. The sermon will discuss some phase
of the commencement theme: standards of success,
looking at life in its entirety, making wise decisions regarding the future, seeking the help of God in all that

one does. This is another way in which Protestantism brings the common life into the church for religious celebration.

This interest of the Protestant Church in the common life is often expressed in another Sunday during the spring, known as Vocation Day. Upon that occasion one of the basic vocations of the community is celebrated during the service. Sometimes members representing a vocation will attend Divine Worship in a body. The theme of their life work is introduced into the liturgy through the Scripture lessons, hymns and anthems and the sacrament of the Word. One year, for example, the First Methodist Church of Evanston had members of the police and fire departments present and the service gave recognition to those areas of the common life in which the whole community is involved. One Sunday the First Unitarian Church of Chicago used Vocation Day to honor the teachers of the community in the service. Dr. Von Ogden Vogt prepared a fine responsive Psalm of Labor which was read from one of the bays of the church, over which was the shield with the symbol of education upon it in bas-relief. In addition, such words as this versicle were used:

- "So is the teacher, instructing the young, Loving wisdom, imparting the spirit of truth."

The choir sang a carol of service and an anthem built around the theme of wisdom. Dr. Vogt preached on the topic, "The Schoolhouse and the Nation." Present in the service were members from the major teacher groups of the metropolitan areas of Chicago.

• festivals of the deity

In the late spring two festivals of the Deity are always celebrated. Since there are only four festivals of the Deity, namely, Christmas, Easter, Pentecost and Trinity, these last two days are of great importance to the church. The date of Pentecost is always dependent upon the date of Easter for it comes seven weeks after the Festival of the Resurrection. It is the day when the Church remembers that amazing moment when the Apostles were gathered in the upper room in Jerusalem during the Jewish Festival of the Passover and were visited by a mighty release of power from God. God in action in the minds of men is known in Christian theology as the Holy Spirit. It seemed to the Apostolic group that living tongues of fire played upon the head of every person present, uniting them into the solidarity of the church and giving them a sense of power and confidence that enabled them to evangelize the world. No wonder that the church observes this day year after year as its birthday. Because the generous gift of God's presence initiated the Christian fire and conserved it, the church calls its birthday the Festival of the Holy Spirit. That is the proper festival designation for Pentecost.

Upon that day very early the church looked forward to the baptism of its candidates for membership. This was the sacramental means of entrance into the church.

Later on when the additional rite of confirmation had been developed, Pentecost was also used for the confirmation of the faith of people by the action of the Holy Spirit of God during this important festival. In many parish churches the candidates for membership would dress in white gowns. In England, therefore, this Sunday of baptism and confirmation was called White Sunday, the term later shortened to Whitsunday. That is why this festival is known by several names, any one of which is now considered correct: Pentecost, Whitsunday or the Festival of the Holy Spirit.

Since the Protestant Church began to observe a full liturgical calendar, theologically acceptable to it, Whitsunday has been a popular festival. Of course, the Lutheran and Episcopal churches always observed the day but it is new to the freer bodies of Protestantism. Several observances are now held upon that day. Often baptism and confirmation are celebrated. Often, too, the parish uses Whitsunday as the occasion of one of its celebrations of Holy Communion. Here is a service which all bodies of Christendom have in common. No matter what their other liturgical practices may be, the structure of their service of Holy Communion is always much the same. The core of the service is the consecration and consumption of bread and wine, symbols of the body and blood of Christ. Each parish church, in celebrating Holy Communion, therefore, on this birthday of the church catholic, has a real sense of its fellowship and solidarity with universal Christendom. Since Whitsunday is a festival day, Holy Communion

is celebrated with color, light and glorious music.
When the service is sung, often a thrilling choral setting is used to bring the day to festival expression.

At the heart of the service is often that ancient hymn,
either sung or read responsively, known as the Veni,
Creator Spiritus, the words of which bring back the
memory of that historic Pentecost so full of the compulsion of God. Again, God's flaming presence seems
to take possession of the congregation as the words
glow with present life:

· Come, Holy Ghost, our souls inspire,
And lighten with celestial fire.

Thou the anointing Spirit art,
Who dost thy sevenfold gifts impart.

Thy blessed unction from above,
Is comfort, life ,and fire of love.

Enable with perpetual light
The dullness of our blinded sight.

Anoint and cheer our soiled face
With the abundance of thy grace.

Keep far our foes; give peace at
home;

Where thou art guide, no ill can
come.

Teach us to know the Father, Son,
And thee, of both, to be but One;

the spring cycle

That through the ages all along,
This may be our endless song:

Praise to thy eternal merit,
Father, Son, and Holy Spirit. Amen.

The Sunday after Pentecost is known as the Festival of the Holy Trinity. This was a late addition to the calendar of worship. It was introduced by the Roman Church in the twelfth century. It is the day when we give special recognition to the trinitarian nature of our faith. The doctrine of the Holy Trinity often confused not only the ordinary layman of the church but also the theologians. The bigger their books seeking to explain the Trinity, the more confused their thinking often proved to be. Intelligent Christians, however, know that the doctrine of the Trinity is merely an inadequate attempt on the part of man to set forth the infinite mystery and richness of the Divine Being. He can never be fully comprehended by man. His nature must always be set forth in something of a symbolic way. The church has chosen the symbolism of the Trinity as its method of understanding the immense transcendence of God. On Trinity Sunday, therefore, hymns and anthems support this concept and sermons seek to explain it.

The sermonic explanation of the Holy Trinity may flow into an outline like this:

The Holy Trinity is an attempt on the part of the Christian religion to explore and define the complex nature of God. It is, of course, only a gesture in the right direction for human beings alive upon the earth

· 127

cannot hope to understand and to reflect all of the mysteries of the Godhead.

The Trinity defines God as Father, Son and Holy Spirit.

When we think of God as the creator of the universe and the will and energy which now sustain it, we call him Father.

When we think of God's attempt to speak to man in history, we remember that he became incarnate in Jesus of Nazareth. Only through a man could God speak to other men; only through a man could the love and compassion of God come to expression. Jesus is the word of God spoken to mankind in history.

When we think of God as the spiritual presence impinging upon our minds today, we call him Holy Spirit. The Holy Spirit is simply another term for God's presence in the world today, the presence which is particularly interested in sharpening the conscience and leading it to Christ.

The days following Trinity Sunday are known as Trinitytide in the Lutheran and Episcopal churches and in those Protestant churches which follow that tradition. The calendar of the National Council of Churches of Christ, however, uses the old pattern and calls these Sundays the Sundays after Pentecost. At any rate, during the late spring and early summer there is opportunity fully to express the richness of God set forth in his extension through the Holy Spirit which manifested itself upon Pentecost and in the Church's doctrine of the Trinity.

In this way the rich and lyrical season of spring

the spring cycle

comes to a close in the Protestant Church. It brought to the congregation three of the major festivals of the church year. Hearts are grateful for the glory and splendor, the hope and support which it brings to mankind.

Eternal Father

of the seasons, we thank Thee now that April has come. Through the long winter months, sometimes filled with uncertainty and anxiety, with pain and despair, we have awaited the coming of this beautiful time. Streaming through the misty dawns of these April days is Thy radiant sun of warmth, bringing to life again the waiting, growing world. Beautiful again is every budding tree, every pale green shoot that rises toward Thee from the ground, every star that quietly appears to lighten these evenings of spring.

Long have we awaited the coming of this beautiful time. Now we believe that Thou wilt bless us again and cause us to enter upon a new beginning that shall wonderfully enrich our lives. Now wilt Thou awaken within us new capacities for thought and action, new insight into the meaning and possibility of our own lives, new courage to meet life bravely and beautifully and triumphantly. Here in this moment of new beginnings, surrounded by every budding tree and plant, and undergirded by Thy mighty and loving help, enable us to sever those ties which have kept us from living abundantly. Enable us now in faith and love to take those great goods, those opportunities for significant experience, those healing gifts which Thou hast prepared for us.

O merciful Father in heaven, support us always, we beseech Thee, with Thy everlasting Presence. Surround us with the fellowship and affection of those who care for us greatly. Make bright the future; strengthen the hope in our hearts, and bring to fine fulfillment those dreams and purposes that are in harmony with Thy holy will; through Jesus Christ our Lord.

Amen.

· **the summer cycle**

The summer cycle of worship varies greatly in Protestant churches. Apparently, some congregations assume that Almighty God is off on a vacation himself for those congregations close the church for the summer, thus giving the impression that God has abdicated and has no further use for the worship of the church. This practice was more common a few years ago than it is today. Churches are now more inclined to treasure the ancient pattern and concept of perpetual prayer and worship arising from the faithful to God from all parts of the world all hours of the day and all days of the week.

In some parts of the country church attendance actually increases during the summer season. This is particularly true in the well known vacation spots where summer visitors help to swell the chorus of amens and hallelujahs in the local parish church. Even special additions are made to the services in these churches placed among the vacation spots of our land. One church beside a northern lake, for example, organized a choric reading group to give additional interest and beauty to the summer service. In addition to the choral music, this speaking choir rhythmically chanted or read some of the great psalms and prophetic passages and suitable contemporary poetry during the service. Oftentimes choirs are enlarged by summer visitors interested in choral music, altars are beautifully decorated with summer flowers and even well known ministers from the cities are brought in as guest preachers to make the services more interesting and attractive.

· independence day

A few points of festival interest give an emotional and liturgical lift to the summer season. Independence Day is one such point of interest. The birth of the nation is bound to have religious significance. We may truthfully say that the United States was founded and developed upon faith in God. The religious tradition is fundamental to our history and can be traced through all of its pages. To repeat the story of the colonies is to say what every school boy knows. The colonies were peopled by men and women who were engaged, not only in an economic undertaking, but also in a religious venture. Even such a commercial venture as the Virginia colony included a paragraph in its charter regarding the propagation of Christianity.

Beautiful in its simplicity is the Mayflower compact, "In the name of God. Amen. We, whose names are underwritten, the loyal subjects of our dread sovereign lord, King James—having undertaken for the glory of God and advancement of the Christian faith and honor of our king and country, a voyage to plant the first colony . . ." These pilgrims, who drew up that Mayflower compact, knew that the success of their venture depended upon the support of Almighty God.

Even more specific in its ascription to Deity is the first constitution of Connecticut, adopted in 1639 and containing sentences like these: "For as much as it hath pleased Almighty God, by the wise disposition of his Divine Providence, so to order and dispose of things that we, the inhabitants of Windsor, Hartford and Wethersfield are now dwelling upon the river of Connecticut . . . and well knowing where the people are gathered together the word of God requires them to maintain the peace . . . we do enter into combination and confederation together to maintain and preserve the liberties and purity of the Gospel of our Lord Jesus which we now profess."

When the final document was written that set the bells of liberty swinging the writers of the Declaration of Independence remembered the religious heritage of the colonists, "We, therefore, the representatives of the United States of America in General Congress, Assembled, appealing to the Supreme Judge of the world for the rectitude of our intentions . . . and for the support of this Declaration, with a firm reliance on the protection of Divine Providence, we mutually pledge to each other our lives, our fortunes and our sacred honor."

We could continue to quote from the basic documents of the American people, including the addresses of George Washington and other presidents which set forth the faith of the American people in the guidance and providence of God. Our fathers believed that God was a participant in the American struggle for freedom. This has been a continuing tradition. Because of it, the Protestant Church, year after year, has celebrated the religious significance of Independence Day on the Sunday nearest to July 4.

• kingdomtide

The last Sunday in August has been designated by the Commission on Worship of the former Federal Council of Churches of Christ as the Festival of Christ the King. This celebration is devoted to the idea of Jesus Christ as King and Lord of mankind. It has its scriptural basis in such passages as Philippians 2 in which Paul says, "Wherefore, God also hath highly exalted him, and given him a name which is above every name: That at the name of Jesus every knee should bow, of things in heaven, and things in earth, and things under the earth; and that every tongue should confess that Jesus Christ is Lord, to the glory of God the Father." Such hymns are sung as "All hail the power of Jesus' name," or "Crown Him with many crowns, the Lamb upon the throne."

It must be said, however, that this particular festival is not widely observed as yet. Its use does not emerge naturally out of Protestant practice and, therefore, it may be sometime before summer congregations will be celebrating this additional festival of the Deity.

The Festival of Christ the King opens the general

season of Kingdomtide. It is an addition to the church year made by the American Protestant Church. Kingdomtide is a formulated word to emphasize Christian interest in the Kingdom of God on the earth. Its Scriptural basis is set forth in Jesus' mission recorded by Mark, "Jesus came into Galilee, preaching the gospel of the kingdom of God and saying, the time is fulfilled, and the kingdom of God is at hand: repent ye, and believe the gospel." In additional passages the nature and pattern of life in the kingdom of God is set forth. The Sermon on the Mount, recorded by Matthew, is typical of these passages. We think of such affirmations of the good life as those crystallized by the Beatitudes, by the Golden Rule and by Jesus' imperative suggestion that we establish patterns of cooperation and loving kindness with all people, including our enemies.

In these emphases, the Church, in recent years, has been tremendously concerned. The whole movement, known as the Social Gospel Movement, goes back to the interest of Walter Rauschenbusch in the relationship of Jesus' ethical teachings to our social order today. Very early in the century the leading Protestant churches began to publish social creeds in which resolutions, formulated by their general assemblies, set forth the position of the church on such topics as public morals, war and peace, economics, labor and management and other phases of our social life. One such creed emphasized the historic interest of the Methodist Church in these areas of living by saying, "The interest of the Methodist Church in social welfare springs from the labors of John Wesley who ministered to the physical, intellectual and social needs of the people to whom he preached the gospel of redemption."

For this emphasis during Kingdomtide there are abundant liturgical materials. In many a Protestant church religion comes alive at the point of its application to some social problem which, when solved religiously, will make the world a better place in which to live. Many a congregation will repeat one of the great prayers of Walter Rauschenbusch from his anthology, "Prayers of the Social Awakening." Many litanies of labor, many prayers for a just and lasting peace, many responsive readings setting forth the aspirations of men in their hope for a better social order are available for us in our Protestant churches. Great hymns are sung during Kingdomtide such as:

> •   "God the Omnipotent! King who ordainest
> Thunder Thy clarion, the lightning Thy
>   sword;
> Show forth Thy pity on high where Thou
>   reignest,
> Give to us peace in our time, O Lord."

One of the most famous hymns for use during Kingdomtide is Frank Mason North's great hymn:

> •   "Where cross the crowded ways of life,
> Where sound the cries of race and clan,
> Above the noise of selfish strife,
> We hear Thy voice, O Son of man!"

When these hymns are sung, these prayers repeated and sermons preached which speak about the election, the current strike, the opportunity of the United Nations and other such topics, Protestant congregations tingle with the good feeling that religion, after all, is interested in something more than the celebration

.   "Of old, unhappy, far-off things,
And battles long ago."

They know that religion is relevant to life and has a clear word concerning it.

The second Sunday of Kingdomtide is known as Labor Sunday. Like Catholic Christianity itself, Protestant churches have always been interested in labor. Way back in Scrooby the early pilgrims were craftsmen and laborers who took their tools over to Holland and who set sail in the Mayflower in order to settle down in New England to continue their labor. In eighteenth century England John Wesley's Methodist revival began among the laboring classes of England. Because he was interested in their welfare and, in addition to his prayers and sermons, sought to bring them patterns of action that would give them better economic security and wider social fellowship, his movement swept England like a great fire. Religion was made relevant again to the working man.

It is part of the celebration of life and religion to sanctify, through worship, the means by which we labor for our daily bread. Summer's close brings a Labor Day service. The following topics are given sermonic consideration: What is the religious basis for effective relations between management and labor?

What are some of the great purposes for which man will take up his tools and work? How can a man make his job increasingly creative? How does man function as one of God's stewards when he works conscientiously at his job? All of these topics and many others are developed by Protestant preachers when Labor Day Sunday comes around.

Summer's end brings us to the close of the cycle of worship in our Protestant churches. How comprehensive in its scope this cycle has been! It has brought into the orbit of prayer and adoration all the civic festivals such as Labor Day, Thanksgiving Day, New Year's Day and Memorial Day. It has included such abiding experiences of man as his spring planting and his harvest. It has followed the interest of the world in Jesus from the first anticipation of his coming, celebrated during Advent, to his Holy Nativity, through his ministry, during his passion, the glorious moment of his resurrection and his coming again to the church at Pentecost. Every fundamental interest in life is brought by the Protestant Church into the magnificent liturgy of the church year.

When we think of the glory of this worship arising to God from all parts of the world throughout the year, we are reminded of the superb words of the Te Deum laudamus:

> We praise thee, O God: we acknowledge thee to be the Lord.
> All the earth doth worship thee: the Father everlasting.

the summer cycle

To thee all Angels cry aloud: the
    Heavens, and all the Powers therein;
To thee Cherubim and Seraphim:
    continually do cry,
Holy, Holy, Holy: Lord God of Sabaoth;
Heaven and earth are full of the Majesty:
    of thy glory,
The glorious company of the Apostles:
    praise thee.
The goodly fellowship of the Prophets:
    praise thee.
The noble army of Martyrs praise thee.
The holy church throughout all the world:
    doth acknowledge thee;
The Father: of an infinite Majesty.

Almighty God,

our heavenly Father, with joyous hearts we worship Thee at the close of the summer season. Beautiful was Thy presence through the golden days and the shimmering, misty nights. Day after day declared Thy glory and the whole earth spoke of Thy handiwork.

While we worship Thee in spirit and truth and gratitude, a hundred different memories of Thy summer glory crowd into our minds again: the long sweep of the beach, the drift wood as white as a skull, the lavish wash of sunlight on sparkling sand, the healing music of the waves which wash and wash against the waiting shore, and the wonderfully generous reach of the sea toward illimitable horizons.

We rejoice again in the pattern of the countryside, in the brown and yellow stubble of the fields where the grain has been cut, in the great purple blanket of a clover field, in the undulating motions of the corn when the wind touches its leaves of green, in red barns that cling to hillsides and white roads that lead to home.

We remember Thy presence, O God, in the cool shade and odor of the pine trees, in the mysterious and comforting music when Thy gentle winds brushed their chiming branches. We remember Thy splendor when lightning tore across the sky and all the trees sang mighty hallelujahs to praise Thy holy name.

O Thou wonderful God, who dost touch us all with the power and beauty of Thy presence, accept our praise and grant us Thy benediction; through Jesus Christ our Lord.

Amen.

index

A

B

index

Tittle, E. F., 27, 49, 109, 120
Trinitytide, 21, 127-128

U

United States, 132, 134
Universal Bible Sunday, 55-56

V

Veni, Creator Spiritus, 126
Vocation Day, 123
Vogt, Von Ogden, 123

W

Washington, George, 34, 76, 133
Watch Night Service (see New Year)
Week of Prayer, 74-75
Wesley, Chas., 54, 65, 107
Wesley, John, 65, 137
White Gift Christmas, 58
Whitsuntide (see Pentecost)
Why the Chimes Rang, 59
Winter, 69
World Communion Sunday, 12, 41-43
World Day of Prayer, 80-81
World Peace Sunday, 50-52

Z

Zwingli, 14, 23

· 148

Date Due